ENOUGH IS ENOUGH

A 150-YEAR PERFORMANCE REVIEW OF THE MINNEAPOLIS POLICE DEPARTMENT

EXPANDED EDITION
SUMMER 2020

CONTENTS

Yes, We Mean Literally Abolish the Police

Because reform won't happen.

The time to abolish the Minneapolis Police Department is now

The Only Solution Is to Defund the Police

The murders of George Floyd and Breonna Taylor prove what we already knew—police "reform" has failed.

The Police Don't Change

Police chiefs may have condemned the killing of George Floyd, but the actions of their officers since show that nothing's shifted.

The answer to police violence is not 'reform'. It's defunding. Here's why

No More Money for the Police

Redirect it to emergency response programs that don't kill black people.

DEFUND THE POLICE NOW

More training, more equipment, and more officers will not stop police from killing Black people.

Movement to defund police gains 'unprecedented' support across US

Cities Ask if It's Time to Defund Police and 'Reimagine' Public Safety

In the wake of George Floyd's killing, some cities are asking if the police are being asked to do jobs they were never intended to do. Budgets are being re-evaluated.

Calls to reform, defund, dismantle and abolish the police, explained.

As some politicians call for reforms in the wake of police brutality protests, residents of some cities are demanding departments be stripped of their budgets or dissolved altogether.

I'm a Minneapolis City Council Member. We Must Disband the Police—Here's What Could Come Next

'You Can Only Demean People So Much.' Minneapolis Activists Aren't Surprised a National Movement Started There

Mpls City Council publicly commits to dismantling police department

Minneapolis Public Schools severs ties to MPD

St. Paul school board votes police out of schools after pressure from students of color

University of Minnesota Ending Contracts With Minneapolis Police Department After George Floyd's Death

First Avenue, Walker Art Center, schools: List cutting ties with MPD grows

What a World Without Cops Would Look Like

"Can we come up with a situation where there are fewer killings, and fewer collateral consequences?"

A New World Is Possible: Defund Police And Fund Black Lives

Minneapolis Had This Coming

My hometown faces not just a rebuilding but a reckoning.

How Defund and Disband Became the Demands

Policing Has Failed: For Real Public Safety, We Need A Million Community-Driven Experiments

Uprisings Are Driving a Surge in Mutual Aid in Minneapolis and Beyond

Minneapolis Organizers Are Already Building the Tools for Safety Without Police

After four nights without police presence, neighborhoods protect themselves

Days of violence and damage led up to Saturday.

Anything feels possible in this moment

FOREWORD TO THE 2020 EXPANDED EDITION

This new, expanded version of the "Enough Is Enough" report was scheduled to be released in spring of 2020. On May 25, 2020, George Floyd was murdered by three Minneapolis police officers as one stood guard.

The writing in this report was done primarily between 2016 and 2019, and was first released in 2017. This expanded edition is being released in summer 2020, while the shockwaves from the May uprising are still spreading. We don't know when you'll be reading this, but we know that our city will never be the same.

As a city, our grief, our rage, our fire, and our frustration are expressions of deep truths. We acknowledge that none of them are new; Black, brown, and Indigenous peoples have carried the oppressive weight of this racist system, and the violence of its police enforcers, since the beginning. We also acknowledge that our connection, our love, our determination, and our solidarity are also our truths, are also necessary, and light our path ahead.

While the police have cracked down on protesters, and the media has focused on riots, looting, and property destruction, Minneapolis community members have engaged in a stunning range of mutual aid efforts: donation drives, community protection/patrols, volunteer cleanups, and neighbors just helping out and looking out for one another. We're not just imagining our police-free future; we're actively building it.

This is bigger than policy. George Floyd deserves to have his humanity honored, and his family supported. At Floyd's memorial, his brother, Philonise Floyd, said, "All these people came to see my brother. And that's amazing to me that he touched so many people's hearts. Because he's been touching our hearts." We fight for abolition because George Floyd, and every victim of the violence and racism inherent in prisons and policing, are human beings, and they matter.

Abolition isn't just about getting rid of prisons and police. It's about what we build in the space they leave behind.

MPD150's work has been primarily focused on narrative: our intention was to tell a story. That story, which will come to life as you read this report, centers on the idea that a world without police isn't just possible, but necessary.

We went into this work knowing that stories generally take time to take root. You plant an idea, give it water, sunlight, and nutrients from the soil, and it grows. What we didn't count on was how eager our community would be to provide those elements; how quickly that story would grow. To be sure, it's a powerful story. It is a story supported by decades of scholarship and vision (especially from Black women like Angela Davis, Ruth Wilson Gilmore, Mariame Kaba, and beyond), a story deeply rooted in the lived experience of the communities that policing was designed to punish and control, but which is often distorted and obscured by the false promises of police reform and "community policing."

Over the past few weeks, city council members in our city have been using explicitly abolitionist rhetoric, saying things like "The department is irredeemably beyond reform," and "Our attempts at incremental reform of policing have failed. We need deep, structural change."

We've been organizers long enough to know that rhetoric isn't the same as action. But we also know that what is said does matter. Language tells a story about what is possible, about what we consider "sensible" or "radical" as we consider policy. Language plants seeds.

Our hope is that this report, and all of the stories held here, will be an instrument of struggle. Here in Minneapolis, we're already seeing organizations like Black Visions Collective and Reclaim the Block carry this narrative into the areas of community organizing and policy, building the momentum and lining up allies to turn narrative into victories. This work is happening here at home, as it happens in communities across—and beyond—the US. As the last headline on the previous page states, "anything feels possible in this moment."

We dedicate this to the elders who got us here, the young Black organizers leading this movement, and everyone doing the hard work of building our present and our future, together.

Previous page: a selection of headlines from both local and national media, May-June, 2020

TO THOSE WHO'VE LED THE WAY

The initiative that we have named MPD150 stands on the shoulders of the activists and organizers, community organizations and street protesters, whistleblowers, families of loved ones lost to police violence, and numerous others who have led the fight for truly safe communities in the past and still today. Their contributions over the years have made this undertaking possible. For this we honor them.

WHO WE ARE

MPD150 is an independent association of organizers, activists, researchers, and artists that came together in the spring of 2016 in anticipation of the Minneapolis Police Department (MPD)'s 150th anniversary. We are not the project of any organization, although we recognize the contributions many of them have made over the years. Some of them have shared leads and material for this report. "Enough Is Enough" is one component of a multi-faceted effort that includes public art, educational activities, political action, cultural activism, and more. We hope to inspire and support new community initiatives that contribute to a shared vision of a police-free future.

TABLE OF CONTENTS

Photo by Annabelle Ma

(c) MPD150 2017; second edition 2020 | ISBN: 978-0-9796104-9-3

Enough Is Enough!

Enough Is Enough! That is both the conclusion and the title of this report, a 150-year performance review of the Minneapolis Police Department (MPD).

The report is the product of an investigation into the conduct of the department over the fifteen decades since its founding in 1867; a survey of its current role and impact especially on marginalized communities; and an exploration of viable alternatives to the policing model. The purpose of this report is to take the idea of police-free communities out of the realm of fantasy and place it firmly in the public agenda as a practical necessity.

Our analysis locates the roots of police brutality, corruption, and racism in its history and founding mission. This is where our attention should be directed, not at frivolous arguments such as whether "all cops are bad." The presence of officers with good intentions, recruits who join the force to make things better, or even reform-minded chiefs does not actually alter the oppressive behavior of police agencies.

The report is organized according to the three areas of focus that have guided its preparation: the past, the present, and the future. This outline is followed, both in the printed version and on MPD150's website, by additional case studies, community interviews, and alternative resources.

The first section will establish that the MPD, far from being an agent of "public safety" or even "law enforcement," has always acted as the enforcement arm of the economic and political elite. Like its fellow departments around the country, it is at the front end of a system of mass incarceration that devours Black, brown and Indigenous peoples, stripping them of voting rights, job prospects, and dignity, keeping wages low and people divided.

The US police system, we contend, is not reformable. Efforts to reform it—aimed at addressing recruitment, training, discipline, oversight, and transparency—are quickly and effectively neutralized by the organized opposition of police departments and their unions and professional associations. In fact, these cycles of reform—looking remarkably the same from one decade to the next—serve to temporarily pacify resistance from victimized communities without altering police business as usual. They also reassure white communities, who are spared the mistreatment directed at their darker-skinned neighbors, and often turn to the police for security. In the short term, reining in police abuse by demanding reforms can provide only limited relief.

Part two speaks of the present. It features interviews by MPD150's interview team and by partner organizations. We share the reflections of professionals (in areas such as mental health, domestic and sexual violence, emergency response, and homelessness) whose work is impacted by the police. They report that the militarized, combative presence of police is not the medicine needed in our traumatized communities. Even the social service functions absorbed into the police system over the years would be better-served by removing them from department control. We also hear from community members who contend with police intervention in their daily lives. The constant reality of intimidation, harassment, and bullying are the wide base of the police misconduct iceberg of which murder by police is just the tip.

In the third section, we turn to face the future. What might it look like if we addressed our communities' needs as neighbors and creative problem solvers instead of relying on force and imprisonment? Here we draw on the insights from our interviews, the promise of existing alternatives, and examples from other places to begin sketching the outlines of the police-free communities of the future. We have no shortage of cultural traditions, innovative social programs, and community resilience strategies from which to draw.

The transition to a resilience-based Minneapolis will not come overnight. It will require a succession of steps that starts with limiting the harm caused daily by police power, and beginning the orderly transfer of resources from the police to projects, programs, and grassroots initiatives that meet people's emergency and long-term needs. Neighborhoods with good jobs, affordable homes, healthy food, and green places to play produce less conflict and fewer mental health crises than ones that feature empty lots, under-funded schools, and starvation wages. Like any process of change, the transitional period will raise new questions and pose new problems. It will, naturally, meet with concerted resistance. The solutions that result, however, will be designed to help all our communities thrive, not contain and divide them.

The material presented here turns the common wisdom on its head. The idea of a police-free future is neither naive nor unrealistic. It is the only pragmatic solution to the challenge of a police system rooted in the era of slavery and Indian removal which has defeated every reform effort thrown at it. To believe that we are just one or two reforms away from turning the police into a trusted partner of the very communities it has treated like enemies to be conquered for a century and a half... that is the ultimate in magical thinking!

It is time for Minneapolis to look this problem in the face and begin a new, more courageous conversation about our future, a conversation that includes possibilities that the police, media pundits, and corporate lobbyists tell us are out of bounds. This report is a contribution to that discussion.

Where We've Been:

A People's History of the Minneapolis Police Department

INTRODUCTION

The Minneapolis Police Department (MPD) was established in 1867, 150 years ago. On the department's website, they describe their mission as: "to protect with courage, to serve with compassion." Unfortunately, they have failed in that mission many times over the last century and a half: even a cursory look at MPD's history reveals patterns of brutality, systemic racism, and failed reform.

In this section of the report, we will examine that history from its beginning, starting with the origins of the concept of policing itself. We'll look at the first fifty years of the Minneapolis Police Department, and the department's early history as a corrupt political tool. Then we'll move into the middle years, 1918 - 1967, and MPD's increasing violence toward Black and Native communities, immigrants, union members, and other marginalized groups. Finally, we'll look at the most recent fifty years—a time of disgrace, militarization, and countless failed reforms at the Minneapolis Police Department.

There are too many stories for us to tell. So much of the story of the Minneapolis Police Department exists not in newspaper clippings and city council records, but in the lived experiences of our communities. We can't possibly provide a full accounting of the harassment and brutality at the hands of the police—too many people have been intimidated into silence or killed for us to tell every story. Even if we could write a comprehensive history of misconduct in the department, it would be too long and too depressing for anyone to read.

But we did our best: over the past year and a half, we've written a collection of more than twenty short pieces on particularly illustrative stories from MPD's history. These pieces served as the basis for the incomplete history we're going to tell here.

If you're interested in learning more about a particular incident in this section, and it has a (!) next to it, that means there's a longer piece about it, including citations, on the timeline section of our website: MPD150.com.

One more note: the past cannot be changed. The weight of the tragedy that the Minneapolis Police Department has caused can't be dismissed. But that doesn't mean there's not hope: in our present and future sections, we'll be discussing the current state of community safety in Minneapolis and how we can strengthen it by building real alternatives to the police. It's up to us to build a way to keep our communities vibrant and healthy. But to imagine where we're going requires an understanding of where we've been. So let's get started.

UNDEVELOPED:
THE ORIGINS OF POLICING

We often talk about police as if they've existed for all of human history, when in reality they're a relatively recent invention. The first modern police force in the world was established in England in the nineteenth century—before that, communities were largely kept safe by informal institutions. In 1829, growing levels of property crime caused by urbanization and the creation of urban poverty led to the creation of a police force in London—the Metropolitan Police Department.[1] Home Secretary Robert Peel was the creator of the department, and based it on the model of the Royal Irish Constabulary, a "peacekeeping" force designed to maintain British rule and control rebellious communities in occupied Ireland. From their very beginnings in London, police departments were rooted in colonialism and the protection of property—policing's origins in the United States, though, are even darker.

Though the thirteen colonies imported a system of elected sheriffs and constables, who were empowered to enforce some laws, formalized American policing really began with slave patrols. Made up of local militias and slaveowners who patrolled the countryside stopping Black people and forcing escaped slaves back into bondage, slave patrols enforced white supremacy from some of the earliest days of the European occupation of the Americas. These patrols (and their Northern equivalents, town watches) were empowered to enforce curfews against Black and Native folks, search and confiscate their property, and brutalize them, with or without cause.[2] These groups were gradually granted additional powers and jurisdiction, eventually evolving directly into modern police departments. One example of this can be seen in Charleston, South Carolina, where a town watch created in 1671 for the explicit purpose of keeping Native and Black people in line eventually turned into the city's first police department.[3]

The City of Minneapolis wasn't formally established until 1867. Its first leader practically begged for a police force to oversee, saying "a mayor without a police force to appoint and regulate would hardly feel that he was Mayor."[4] The city council agreed, and on March 9, 1867, the first four officers were appointed to the Minneapolis Police Department.

It's important to note the historical context here: the Minneapolis Police

---

1   Kristian Williams, Our Enemies in Blue: Police and Power in America (Baltimore: AK Press, 2015), 59.
2   Kristian Williams, Our Enemies in Blue: Police and Power in America (Baltimore: AK Press, 2015), 74.
3   Ibid. 75 - 77.
4   Ibid.

Department was established less than thirty years after Dred Scott and his wife Harriet were held as slaves at Fort Snelling,[5] only five years after the hanging of thirty-eight Dakota men at the hands of the US government following the US Dakota War of 1862, only two years after the end of the Civil War.

Perhaps, given the department's beginnings, the history that was to follow was predictable.

UNPROFESSIONAL:
MPD, 1867 - 1917

In its early years, the Minneapolis Police Department grew rapidly, with each new mayor appointing more officers to the police force as the city population skyrocketed. At the time, mayors were elected annually, and often the entire police department would change every year as the new mayor fired their political opponents and appointed their friends, family, and political supporters to police jobs,[6] a common practice across the country at the time.[7] These early police were completely untrained, didn't wear uniforms, and drank on duty so often that in 1875, the city council ordered the mayor to prohibit police from entering saloons while on duty except for when they were conducting official business.[8] Often the laws that were enforced changed from year to year as well, particularly those around sex work: although brothels were mostly allowed to operate without too much trouble, the first fines were imposed upon "the women of the town" in 1878. In the first year alone, the city collected $3,470 in fines from sex workers (more than $80,000 in 2017 dollars).[9]

The city workhouse was completed in

1886. Though the 13th amendment, ratified in 1865, prohibited chattel slavery, it allowed for involuntary servitude "as a punishment for crime,"[10] and the city made huge profits out of that loophole. The city forced inmates to do a variety of work, including farming, making clothing, and working in the city quarry. In the first four years alone, the city made almost $9,000 ($244,000 in 2017 dollars) from inmate labor.[11] Early Minneapolis had even more brutal ways of dealing with crime, too: the city's first hanging was held in 1882.[12]

By 1889, the police force had grown to 169 uniformed officers patrolling a city of 200,000 people.[13] That year, tensions between industrialist Thomas Lowry and streetcar workers erupted into a massive fifteen-day strike, with strikers and strikebreakers brawling for control of the streets. The Minneapolis Police Department came down hard on the strikers, arresting dozens and helping Lowry break the strike while avoiding offering any concessions to his workers.

By 1900, Doctor A. A. Ames had been elected to his fourth term as mayor of Minneapolis. Unlike in his first three terms, this time Ames decided to use his political power for personal gain. He appointed his brother, Fred Ames, to be the chief of police, and quickly turned the Minneapolis Police Department into one of the most effective tools for corruption in the city. Under Ames, MPD officers committed graft, extortion, and burglaries, finally being stopped by a group of civilian activists in 1902. MPD wasn't the only problematic department at the time—many early police departments were deeply complicit in corrupt political machines[14]—but it did become infamous across the nation for the boldness of its crimes (!).

The department continued developing into the twentieth century: in 1902, five police precincts were established, and in 1909, the department bought its first paddy wagon, which helped the department round up "undesirables" under the state's recently passed vagrancy laws.[15]

At the turn of the century, MPD often used its increasing power on behalf of the Citizens' Alliance, a far right group of powerful businessmen established in 1903. The Citizens' Alliance used MPD to harass, infiltrate, and attack labor groups, preventing them from building political power and organizing unions.[16] The 1889 streetcar strike already provided one example of how to use violence to force workers into obedience, and the 1909 Machinists' Strike provided another: police protected strikebreakers as they crossed picket lines, and helped crush the strike without any compromise on behalf of employers.[17]

Despite their frequent mobilization against labor organizers, Minneapolis police officers established their own union, the Police Officers Federation of Minneapolis, in 1916,[18] and were eventually welcomed into the American Federation of Labor.[19] As the Minneapolis Police Department drew close to its fifty-year anniversary in 1917, the department numbered more than 300 officers, without training, exerting power and control over a city of more than 300,000 residents.[20,21] In its first fifty years, MPD generated wealth for the city, shut down several massive strikes, and was deeply implicated in the corrupt administration of Mayor Ames. If anything, the next fifty years would be even worse.

5   "Slavery at Fort Snelling (1820s - 1850s)," Historic Fort Snelling, accessed November 03, 2017, http://www.historicfortsnelling.org/history/slavery-fort-snelling.
6   Michael Fossum, History of the Minneapolis Police Department, (Minneapolis, Minn.: s.n., 1996), 1.
7   Kristian Williams, Our Enemies in Blue: Police and Power in America (Baltimore: AK Press, 2015), Chapter 3.
8   Augustine Costello, History of the Fire and Police Departments of Minneapolis (Minneapolis, MN: The Relief Association, 1890), 252.
9   Augustine Costello, History of the Fire and Police Departments of Minneapolis (Minneapolis, MN: The Relief Association, 1890), 261.
10   U.S. Constitution, Amendment XIII
11   Minneapolis Police Department, 1872 - 1973: 101 Years of Service (1973), 8.
12   Ibid. s, 9.
13   Michael Fossum, History of the Minneapolis Police Department, (Minneapolis, Minn.: s.n., 1996), 3.
14   Kristian Williams, Our Enemies in Blue: Police and Power in America (Baltimore: AK Press, 2015), 89 - 100
15   Michael Fossum, History of the Minneapolis Police Department, (Minneapolis, Minn.: s.n., 1996), 4.
16   William Millikan, A Union against Unions: the Minneapolis Citizens Alliance and its Fight against Organized labor, 1903-1947 (St. Paul: Minnesota Historical Society Press, 2001), xxvii.
17   Ibid., 37.
18   "History," Police Officers Federation of Minneapolis, accessed November 01, 2017, http://www.mpdfederation.com/about-us/history/.
19   William Millikan, A Union against Unions: the Minneapolis Citizens Alliance and its Fight against Organized labor, 1903-1947 (St. Paul: Minnesota Historical Society Press, 2001), 206.
20   Michael Fossum, History of the Minneapolis Police Department, (Minneapolis, Minn.: s.n., 1996), 12.
21   "Minneapolis, Minnesota Population History 1880 - 2016." Minneapolis, Minnesota Population History | 1880 - 2016. October 3, 2017. Accessed October 31, 2017. https://www.biggestuscities.com/city/minneapolis-minnesota.

UNRESTRAINED:
MPD, 1917 - 1967

The Minneapolis Police Department became larger, more sophisticated, and increasingly brutal as the 1920s approached. By this time, the Citizens' Alliance was a deeply entrenched force in Minneapolis politics, and they continued to use MPD and other law enforcement agencies to push their anti-union agenda. In 1917, supposedly looking to support troops fighting in World War I, the Citizens' Alliance formed their own private army, fully supported by local law enforcement. When another streetcar strike broke out in 1917, the Hennepin County Sheriff's Office quickly deputized the private army and deployed it onto Minneapolis streets. With the Citizens' Alliance troops armed with rifles and bayonets, the strikers didn't stand a chance, and were quickly defeated.[22]

In other arenas of community control, the Minneapolis Police Department was much less effective: during prohibition (1920 - 1933), MPD attempted to arrest community members for possession of alcohol, but was often held back by the Minnesota Supreme Court. The Court refused to uphold convictions of alcohol possession; only those directly involved in the sale of liquor were punished.[23]

Meanwhile, a deep and unrelenting strain of white supremacy was growing stronger in Minneapolis and across the state. The Klu Klux Klan established more than fifty chapters across Minnesota beginning in 1917, and a growing Black population in Minneapolis was subject to racism of many varieties.[24] Police brutality was a constant threat to the Minneapolis Black community of the 1920s.

On June 20, 1922, MPD officers savagely beat and arrested four men for allegedly inviting some white women to a dance. That same day, an officer tried to shoot a Black man in the Mill City district after he refused to "move on," only to be disarmed by the man, who ran from the scene with the officer's gun. Members of the Black community, notably the Minneapolis NAACP, mobilized to demand reform of the Minneapolis Police Department. The calls for police accountability were largely ignored, and racism in MPD continued to be a major problem (!).

The Citizens' Alliance continued to mold the Minneapolis Police Department into a more effective tool to do their bidding; in the mid 1920s, they waged a public relations war against the police union, pressuring officers to say whether their loyalties lay with the American Federation of Labor or the city government. In 1926, the police union severed their ties once and for all with the national labor movement, a separation that remains to this day.[25]

The late 1920s led to other changes in the department as well; the first MPD training ever was held in 1929, sixty-two years after the establishment of the department.[26] The training was indicative of a larger trend across the country: professionalization, where police departments worked hard to establish the idea that they were the foremost experts on crime prevention in the community.[27] At the time, the entire police academy consisted of a day or two of lectures—hardly enough to make anyone a "professional."

The police were experts, however, at fighting labor movements, and they had another chance to demonstrate their skills in the 1930s. In 1934, five years into the Great Depression, unions were starting to gain a foothold in Minneapolis. On May 16, 1934, thousands of truck drivers went on strike as part of the Teamsters union, leading to months of protests, negotiations, and street fighting in Minneapolis. In response, the Minneapolis Police Department, along with the Hennepin County Sheriff, deputized hundreds of civilians aligned with the Citizens' Alliance and encouraged them to use violence against strikers. The deputies were poorly trained and armed, and were defeated by the strikers in a massive battle downtown. This didn't stop MPD from trying to end the strike; on July 20, they ambushed a group of seventy strikers, shooting them in the back with shotguns as they ran away and killing two of them. In the end, the strikers won the right to form a union, and the Minneapolis Police Department's streak of successfully crushing strikes was broken (!).

When the United States entered World War II in 1941, the Minneapolis Police Department quickly took on the role of controlling public opinion. Working with J. Edgar Hoover and his recently formed Federal Bureau of Investigation, MPD established the Internal Security Division to gather intelligence on the people of Minneapolis. The ISD's duties included investigating people who might be subversive, confiscating contraband equipment, and resettling Japanese and German nationals who were paroled from internment camps. At one point, anti-immigrant sentiments led to MPD regularly "checking on" over 10,000 "enemy aliens."[28] The fears that led to this political witch hunt were completely unfounded—"enemy aliens" living in the United States didn't take a single life throughout the whole war.

The 1960s led to a host of changes in the department. From 1960 to 1965, MPD hired more than 150 new officers and civilian staff, increasing its total size to 809 employees.[29] They also created a number of new departments, including a narcotics unit and an early form of SWAT team known as the "Special Operations Division."[30] In 1966, they also established the school liaison program, known today as the School Resource Officer program, to "create a favorable rapport between the juvenile community

22   William Millikan, A Union against Unions: the Minneapolis Citizens Alliance and its Fight against Organized labor, 1903-1947 (St. Paul: Minnesota Historical Society Press, 2001), 125-126
23   Michael Fossum, History of the Minneapolis Police Department, (Minneapolis, Minn.: s.n., 1996), 4.
24   Johnson, Kay. "When the Klan came to Minnesota." Crow River Media, (October 24, 2013) Accessed November 01, 2017. http://www.crowrivermedia.com/hutchinsonleader/news/lifestyle/when-the-klan-came-to-minnesota/article_a08b3390-cf3d-5419-afc6-486ac0e63475.html.
25   William Millikan, A Union against Unions: the Minneapolis Citizens Alliance and its Fight against Organized labor, 1903-1947 (St. Paul: Minnesota Historical Society Press, 2001), 206 - 207
26   Minneapolis Police Department, 1872 - 1973: 101 Years of Service (1973), 29.
27   Kristian Williams, Our Enemies in Blue: Police and Power in America (Baltimore: AK Press, 2015), 212.
28   Michael Fossum, History of the Minneapolis Police Department, (Minneapolis, Minn.: s.n., 1996), 5.
29   Ibid., 7.
30   Ibid., 20, 22.

and the police department."[31] Of course, the school liaison program ignored the real problem—in many cases, students didn't have a "favorable rapport" with the police because officers were brutal, unaccountable, and racist.

Tension between the Black community and the police was a constant in midcentury Minneapolis. Black people were systematically excluded from every part of the city except for the north side, denied access to well-paying jobs, blocked from homeownership, and routinely attacked by police officers. The Black community's frustration with white supremacy came to a head in two riots on Plymouth Avenue: a smaller one in August 1966, and a larger one in July 1967.[32] The first riot was in response to a number of factors including employment discrimination, but the later uprising had one particular cause: police racism.

Over four days in July 1967, police refused to intervene when buses wouldn't bring Black people back to the north side following the Aquatennial parade; police allowed a white crowd to throw glass bottles at a Black crowd; police watched on as a group of four white boys savagely beat a Black boy; and police violently threw Black community members to the ground while breaking up a fight. The community was fed up, and on July 19, 1967, the north side erupted into rioting. The uprising led to a massive police response and the deployment of the National Guard, with several community members arrested (!).

In response to the riots, the mayor proposed a number of police reform initiatives, none of which solved the underlying problems in the department. What neither the mayor nor the community could know was that the pattern established by the 1967 riot—police brutality leads to community outrage, leads to protests, leads to promises of reform, leads to a lack of

meaningful change—would become a constant feature of policing in Minneapolis for the next fifty years.

Unreformable:
MPD, 1967 - 2017

As the 1960s came to a close, demands for police accountability grew louder, and city officials proposed a set of reforms in response. One reform MPD implemented was the "Community Relations Division," a public relations effort to improve the department's image in communities of color through outreach.[33]

Another reform discussion centered around investigating police misconduct. Prior to the late 1960s, there was no formal process for investigating complaints against police officers, and the city scrambled to put one together. In the last few years of the decade, MPD created the Internal Affairs Unit to conduct internal investigations, and the city council created a Civil Rights Commission with the authority to investigate civilian complaints about police officers. Both would become notorious for their inability to hold police accountable for brutality and misconduct (!).

Not everyone had faith that the city's reforms would bear fruit. In 1968, community patrols (the Soul Patrol, Black Patrol, and AIM patrol) emerged in Black and Native communities to keep people safe, deescalate conflict, and prevent police violence. These programs were enormously successful, and their legacies continue today (!).

The Minneapolis Police Department continued its charm offensive into the 1970s, instituting more "community policing" initiatives based on the idea that relationships between communities and the police were bad not because of police misconduct, but because of miscommunication. The MPD programs included the "Model Cities" initiative,

which encouraged officers to get out of their cars and talk with residents, and the Police Resource Team for Education, an effort to get cops into classrooms to talk with students about their work.[34,35]

Meanwhile cops were working to undermine the reforms of the late 1960s. In 1971, Mayor Charles Stenvig, who had previously served as head of the police union, revoked the Civil Rights Commission's authority to investigate complaints against police officers, once again making MPD the only local agency authorized to investigate MPD.[36]

Without real accountability, "police-community relations" efforts did little to repair the relationship between MPD and communities of color. In 1974, the Minnesota Advisory Committee to the US Commission on Civil Rights found that MPD was enforcing laws unfairly in the Native community, and in 1975, eleven incidents of police brutality led the Minnesota Department of Human Rights to begin an investigation of the Minneapolis Police Department, eventually finding that MPD's recruitment and hiring practices were deeply racist. In response to the accusations, the department once again instituted surface-level reforms in their recruitment and training practices, reforms that failed to fix the culture of the department (!).

Throughout the 1970s and 1980s, MPD had a reputation for being one of the most homophobic police departments in the country. MPD harassed queer people, enforced sodomy laws against them, failed to protect them from homophobic violence, and conducted raids on popular gay bathhouses.[37] Though the last raid on a bathhouse occurred on February 10, 1980, police harassment of queer folks remained frequent. In one 1982 example, cops showed up at the Saloon gay bar only to find two homophobes attacking two gay men, who were fighting back. Rather than protecting the gay men, the

31   Ibid., 25-26.
32   Camille Venee, "'The Way Opportunities Unlimited, Inc.': A Movement for Black Equality in Minneapolis, MN 1966-1970" (Honors Thesis, Emory University, 2013, http://pid.emory.edu/ark:/25593/d6v0d)
33   Michael Fossum, History of the Minneapolis Police Department, (Minneapolis, Minn.: s.n., 1996). 7.
34   Michael Fossum, History of the Minneapolis Police Department, (Minneapolis, Minn.: s.n., 1996). 8.
35   Minneapolis Police Department. 1872 - 1973: 101 Years of Service. 1973. Pg. 26
36   The Police Civilian Review Working Committee, A Model for Civilian Review of Police Conduct in Minneapolis: a report to the Mayor and City Council (Minneapolis, MN, 1989).
37   Anthony V. Bouza, Police Unbound: Corruption, Abuse, and Heroism by the Boys in Blue, (Amherst, NY: Prometheus Books, 2001) Ebook locations 2734-2749.

cops arrested them and charged them with assault, disorderly conduct, and resisting arrest (!).

The 1980s didn't bring an improvement in the attitude of the Minneapolis Police Department—if anything, they made it worse. Upon being appointed police chief in 1980, Tony Bouza characterized the department as "damn brutal, a bunch of thumpers."[38] Bouza was hired as a police reformer, but even he later recognized that he had little effect on the culture of the department, describing himself as a "failed police executive" and writing in 2017 that he "did affect their actions...but changed nothing permanently—look around you."[39]

Michael Quinn was a Minneapolis police officer from 1975 to 1999, and has also spoken out about MPD's departmental culture, telling stories of officers drinking on the job, committing burglary, savagely beating sex workers, and more. In each of those cases, the "code of silence" required that officers never report each other's misconduct, and the officers involved went unpunished.[40] Quinn faced his share of derision from officers for violating that code of silence, including threats from current police union head Bob Kroll.[41] As Tony Bouza put it, "the Mafia never enforced its code of blood-sworn omerta with the ferocity, efficacy, and enthusiasm the police bring to the Blue Code of Silence."[42]

By the end of the 1980s, the devastating wars on drugs and gang activity had led to increasingly militarized police departments being turned loose on communities of color. In 1989, this led to a number of tragedies at the hands of the Minneapolis Police Department: the brutal arrest of a group of Black youth at an Embassy Suites downtown, and the deaths of Black elders Lillian Weiss and Lloyd Smalley during a botched SWAT raid (!). The incidents led to a number of protests demanding police accountability, which led to the creation of the Civilian Review Authority (CRA) in 1990. The CRA fared no

Photo by Red Power Media

"In 1968, community patrols (the Soul Patrol, Black Patrol, and AIM patrol) emerged in Black and Native communities to keep people safe, deescalate conflict, and prevent police violence. These programs were enormously successful, and their legacies continue today."

better than its '60s-era predecessor, the Civil Rights Commission, and was ultimately ineffective in holding officers accountable (!).

The newly established Civilian Review Authority wasn't able to prevent a host of tragedies from happening throughout the 1990s as police continued to brutalize communities of color. In late 1990, police killed Tycel Nelson, a Black seventeen-year-old, while he was running away from them, provoking a new round of protests and demands for reform (!). But the relationship between the police and the community was about to get even worse.

On September 25, 1992, Metro Transit police beat an elderly Black man after he paid less than the full fare to ride a bus. Late that night, a group of youth, furious about the man's treatment, ambushed and killed Minneapolis Police Officer Jerry Haaf.[43] The police union took the opportunity to demand more money for drug enforcement and gang control, organizing rallies accusing the police chief, mayor, and city council of causing Haaf's death by being soft on crime. Meanwhile, the Black community was being terrorized—the investigation into Haaf's murder was swift and brutal, targeting many community members who had nothing to do with the shooting.

38   "Drug Enforcement in Minority Communities: The Minneapolis Police Department," Police Executive Research Forum/National Institute of Justice, 1994, p. 7.
39   Tony Bouza, "America's Police Are Still Out Of Control," Southside Pride (Minneapolis), August 21, 2017.
40   Michael Quinn, Walking with the Devil: the Police Code of Silence- the Promise of Peer Intervention, (S.l.: QUINN & ASSOCIATES, 2017) Ebook locations 64-67.
41   Ibid. Ebook location 60.
42   Anthony V. Bouza, Police Unbound: Corruption, Abuse, and Heroism by the Boys in Blue, (Amherst, NY: Prometheus Books, 2001) Ebook location 157.
43   Mel Reeves, "Murder of policeman and beating of blind man shock city." Minneapolis Spokesman, October 1, 1992.

"The Minneapolis Police Department was built on violence, corruption, and white supremacy. Every attempt ever made to reform it or hold it accountable has been soundly defeated.

The culture of silence and complicity in the department, along with the formidable political power wielded by the police union, will continue to preserve the status quo as long as we keep placing our faith in the reforms that have failed us for the last 150 years.

It's time for us to face the reality—if we want to build a city where every community can thrive, it will have to be a city without the Minneapolis Police Department."

The Black community wasn't the only community of color being attacked by MPD in the early '90s—brutality against Native people was also frequent and horrifying. In one case, two passed-out Native men were taken on a "rough ride" in a squad car's trunk in 1993 (!), and in another case the same year, police officers working on a case at the Little Earth community shot a sixteen-year-old playing with a toy gun (!). Another case at Little Earth in 1994 led to community outrage when two MPD officers kidnapped an East African man and tried to extort $300 from him (!).

Misogyny was also a major problem in the Minneapolis Police Department. In September 1994, Officer Michael Ray Parent was charged with felony kidnapping and third-degree sexual assault for forcing a woman to perform oral sex on him to avoid a traffic ticket. Parent was eventually convicted in 1995, the first MPD officer to get sentenced to prison in over twenty years (!).

In 1998, a group of protestors known as the Minnehaha Free State attempted to stop a proposed reroute of Highway 55 that would destroy a site sacred to the Dakota people. Their camp was raided by more than 800 officers, many of them from the Minneapolis Police Department. At the time, it was the largest law enforcement action in state history (!).

The next year, Minnesota State Representative Rich Stanek led an effort to repeal residency requirements for police officers and other public employees around the state. The bill passed, making it illegal for local governments to require that police officers live in the city limits.[44] That law is still in force in 2017, and Representative Stanek has since become Hennepin County Sheriff Stanek.

In 2003, another round of community protests erupted after eleven-year-old Julius Powell was hit by a wayward police bullet on the north side. Community members asked the federal Department of Justice (DOJ) to intervene, and a mediator was sent to Minneapolis to try to resolve the conflict between the community and the police. The DOJ helped to broker a landmark agreement between community members and the police, creating a group called the Police Community Relations Council (PCRC) to try to improve police-community rapport (!). In addition to creating the PCRC, the agreement also required that the police chief institute over a hundred reforms in the department. The PCRC was gradually undermined by the city and forced to disband against their will in 2008. At the time of the PCRC's dissolution, more than forty of the promised reforms remained incomplete.

Even while the PCRC was active, there were a number of egregious incidents of racism by MPD against Minneapolis residents. In 2006, MPD officers beat Juan Vasquez and locked him in a swelteringly hot squad car for more than half an hour (!). Less than two months later, Minneapolis police officers shot and killed nineteen-year-old Fong Lee after chasing him down outside of a school. The officers maintained that Lee had been carrying a gun and posed a threat to officers, but evidence suggested that the gun was actually planted by MPD officers (!).

2007 proved that even some police knew the department had serious problems with racism: that year, five Black police officers, including current MPD Chief Medaria Arradondo, sued the department for racial discrimination, demanding departmental reforms and hundreds of thousands of dollars. The city ended up settling the lawsuit for $2 million—and no reform requirements (!).

In December 2007, the police department showed their reckless disregard for the lives of north side residents again when officers mistakenly executed a "no knock" raid on the house of an innocent Hmong family. Three police officers were nearly killed when the father shot them with a shotgun, assuming they were burglars. Luckily, no one was seriously injured (!).

---

44   Rich Stanek, "Stanek Residency Freedom Bill becomes Law," Representative Rich Stanek Press Release. Accessed March 15, 1999. http://www.house.leg.state.mn.us/GOP/goppress/Stanek/0309rsresidency.htm.

Another major scandal around police conduct came to light in 2009 when it was revealed that an interdepartmental unit called the Metro Gang Strike Force had been surveilling, brutalizing, and stealing from people of color in Minneapolis. The unit was disbanded in the chaos, but none of the officers involved, many of whom worked for MPD, were held accountable for their crimes (!).

The 2010s brought new injustices: unarmed twenty-eight-year-old David Smith was killed by police in September 2010 while having a mental health episode. In November 2010, Jason Yang was found dead under suspicious circumstances following a chase with police officers (!). In 2011, MPD officers helped convict Cece McDonald of manslaughter after she was attacked by a transphobic white supremacist and killed him in self-defense (!).

With incidents of brutality a near constant in Minneapolis, the police union decided there was only one thing to be done: destroy the Civilian Review Authority. In 2012, they went to the state legislature and lobbied successfully for the passage of a bill prohibiting Civilian Review Boards from issuing statements on whether officers had committed misconduct, effectively taking away the limited power they had. In response, the city council moved to create the Office of Police Conduct Review (OPCR), an equally ineffective police review agency based in the city's Civil Rights Department (!).

In 2013, the Minneapolis Police Department killed two people in one afternoon: Terrence Franklin was cornered and shot to death in a South Minneapolis basement, and Ivan Romero was killed less than an hour later when a squad car ran a red light and hit his motorcycle (!).

Meanwhile, MPD was undergoing a public relations makeover: Mayor Betsy Hodges and Police Chief Janee Harteau created yet another civilian oversight group, the Police Conduct Oversight Commission (PCOC), and instituted a program called MPD 2.0

calling for officers to treat community members exactly like they would treat members of their family.[45] Like so many before them, these reforms did little to transform the department; the PCOC's recommendations are largely ignored to this day (!).

2014 saw one of the strangest moments in the history of the department. That year, Mayor Hodges was pushing for body cameras on officers as a solution to police misconduct, a plan that the police union hated. In an attempt to discredit her politically, they fed a story to local news station KSTP that she had been caught throwing gang signs in a photo with a community activist. In reality, the photo just showed the two pointing at each other. The story went viral, and millions around the country got a good laugh out of the absurdity of the claims. But once again, the police union successfully reminded an elected official of their considerable political power (!).

In 2015, Minneapolis police officers shot and killed Jamar Clark, an unarmed Black man, while responding to a 9-1-1 call in north Minneapolis. In response, hundreds of community members occupied Plymouth Avenue outside the Fourth Precinct for 18 days, demanding the release of video footage of the incident and the prosecution of the officers involved (!). Massive mobilizations against police racism continued into 2016 when Philando Castile was murdered by the Falcon Heights Police Department, prompting an occupation of the street outside the Governor's Mansion in St. Paul.

MPD's legacy of corruption, brutality, and murder continued in 2017. Earlier that year, a Minneapolis Police Officer shot and killed Justine Damond, an unarmed Australian woman, after she called 9-1-1 to report a possible sexual assault outside her home. The officers were wearing body cameras, but the cameras hadn't been activated, so the only accounts of the shooting were those of the police officers (!).

Mayor Hodges demanded the resignation of Police Chief Harteau

following the shooting, promoting Medaria Arradondo to become the first Black police chief in the department's history.

But the history of policing in Minneapolis and across the country has taught us that it doesn't matter who the chief is, or even who runs the city: the police can't be controlled. The Minneapolis Police Department was built on violence, corruption, and white supremacy. Every attempt ever made to reform it or hold it accountable has been soundly defeated. The culture of silence and complicity in the department, along with the formidable political power wielded by the police union, will continue to preserve the status quo as long as we keep placing our faith in the reforms that have failed us for the last 150 years. It's time for us to face the reality—if we want to build a city where every community can thrive, it will have to be a city without the Minneapolis Police Department.

Note for the expanded edition: find excerpts from our longer timeline project, along with a separate timeline tool, on pages 74-85.

45   Minneapolis Police Department, MPD 2.0: A New Policing Model (Minneapolis, MN, 2015).

15

THE IDEA OF A POLICE-FREE
FUTURE IS NEITHER NAIVE NOR
UNREALISTIC. IT IS THE ONLY
PRAGMATIC SOLUTION TO THE
CHALLENGE OF A POLICE SYSTEM
ROOTED IN THE ERA OF SLAVERY
AND INDIAN REMOVAL WHICH
HAS DEFEATED EVERY REFORM
EFFORT THROWN AT IT. TO
BELIEVE THAT WE ARE JUST ONE
OR TWO REFORMS AWAY FROM
TURNING THE POLICE INTO A
TRUSTED PARTNER OF THE VERY
COMMUNITIES IT HAS TREATED
LIKE ENEMIES TO BE CONQUERED
FOR A CENTURY AND A HALF...
THAT IS THE ULTIMATE IN MAGICAL
THINKING!

Where We're At:

A Community Report on the Minneapolis Police Department of 2017

This section reviews the present state of policing and features interviews with community members on how the Minneapolis Police Department functions in people's lives today. When it comes to police brutality, the typical response from politicians across the spectrum in Minneapolis is a demand for more cops. Many conservatives call for the hiring of more cops, while many liberals and progressives demand different kinds of reforms. Neither of these responses address police terror at its roots, nor do they address the systemic economic, social, and racial injustice that commonly brings marginalized people into contact with MPD. Mitigating the harm MPD causes is worthwhile. It is dangerous, however, to push the idea that MPD is capable of being reformed, and we will see why this is a false narrative in the following community interviews.

The data, as well as the personal and professional day-to-day experiences of Minneapolis residents, shows us that the idea of community policing is just more lip-service from the establishment.

It is not uncommon for people to respond to the latest police brutality or fatality, such as the homicides by MPD of Terrance Franklin, Fong Lee, Jamar Clark, Justine Damond, and countless others with words like, "but the police are supposed to protect and serve!" Let's take a closer look at the myth that police are here to protect and serve everyone and that police violence is simply the product of a few bad apples that spoil the

barrel of cops. Today, Minneapolis Police Department vehicles deceptively display the words, "to serve with courage, to protect with compassion." That slogan actually came from the marketing company Kazoo when they were hired in 2009 to help clean up the image of the Minneapolis Police Department. The director for the MPD marketing account, Tom DuPont, stated, "Kazoo set out to create recruitment materials that emphasized service. But when the rank-and-file got wind of the new emphasis on 'compassion,' a fairly rough pushback ensued."[1] As an alternative, Kazoo created the line "Be looked up to," which was added to posters that were subsequently distributed in target-market communities via schools, churches, community centers, and more.

This is a good example of how the system protects itself—when confronted with evidence of police terror, the government responds with public relations campaigns. One example of police image management can be seen in the Department of Justice's COPS (Community Oriented Police Services) program, presented in six pillars. These pillars represent the typical public relations-style responses used time and time again to pacify outcries from the community regarding police brutality around the country. One of these pillars is community policing. According to the official US Department of Justice COPS website, "since 1994, the COPS Office has invested more than $14 billion to 'help advance community policing.'[2] Some of this money has been invested

in Minneapolis—we're one of six cities participating in the DOJ's National Initiative of Building Community Trust and Justice. MPD is currently in its third year of the three-year, $4.75 million project. This is just one in a long line of reform programs marketed to "increase trust between communities and the criminal justice system."[3]

These efforts have done little to stop police brutality. 2016 saw an all-time high in deaths caused by police shootings according to the Minnesota Bureau of Criminal Apprehension. The crime index hit a historic low in 2016 that hasn't happened since 1966, and even in densely populated urban areas the violent crime rates by community members have been steadily declining as violent crime committed by MPD continues to rise.[4,5] It's clear that "community oriented policing services" aren't the answer we need.

Even the most helpful statistics fail to fully explain the harm and trauma that the police cause marginalized communities on a daily basis. Instead of trying to speak for the community we've asked the community speak for itself.

1   Mullman., Jeremy. "Minneapolis Police Turn to Branding to Burnish Reputation." Ad Age. February 19, 2009. Accessed November 14, 2017. http://adage.com/article/news/minneapolis-po lice-turn-branding-burnish-reputation/134748/.
2   COPS Office: About COPS. Accessed November 14, 2017. https://cops.usdoj.gov/Default.asp?Item=35.
3   National Initiative for Building Community Trust & Justice. "Minneapolis, Minnesota." Minneapolis, Minnesota. Accessed November 14, 2017. https://trustandjustice.org/pilot-sites/info/minne apolis-minnesota.
4   Gottfried, Mara H., and Josh Verges. "Minnesota shooting deaths by police highest ever recorded. Dangerous year for cops, too." Twin Cities. November 25, 2016. Accessed November 14, 2017 http://www.twincities.com/2016/11/25/minnesota-shooting-deaths-by-police-highest-ever-recorded-dangerous-year-for-cops-too/.
5   Mannix, Andy. "Minnesota crime drops to the lowest rate since The Beatles were bigger than Jesus." MinnPost. July 2, 2015. Accessed November 14, 2017. https://www.minnpost.com/ data/2015/07/minnesota-crime-drops-lowest-rate-beatles-were-bigger-jesus.

The Interviews

Over the last year and a half, MPD150 and community partners have interviewed hundreds of community members about their interactions with the Minneapolis Police Department. These interviews were done with two groups of people: those likely to come into contact with police via their profession—whether employed through Hennepin County, the city of Minneapolis, or nonprofit and grassroots organizations—and those likely to come into contact with the police due to their skin color, social, or economic status. We've included excerpts from these interviews below, and we invite you to read through them, remembering that there is a human story behind every single one.

For the sake of privacy and security, the names of interviewees and identifying information about employers have been changed or omitted.

MPD FUNCTIONS TODAY AS A FORCE THAT DOES NOT PROTECT OR SERVE:

MPD CRIMINALIZES THE COMMUNITY

"The police presence is all over. We have so much surveillance inside and outside of the shelter. We have police officers stationed. Your right to privacy is voided. Everything is set up like a prison. People already feel 'criminalized' and like they are being watched even if they have not committed a crime. People would be more humanized if this presence was voided."

"There is not always an understanding from officers of the financial reasons, children involved, love and affection, and investment involved. Lots of police do not understand why a victim would stay with their abuser. They often get tired of going back to the same house multiple times. It's really disheartening from someone who is supposed to be your partner and out there to serve the community and they have such a harmful attitude. On our hotline we

do not necessarily get all of the calls coming in from Domestic Violence (DV). The police do not contact us every time. When we do get calls from officers, they don't always understand the nuances within DV. A huge piece of DV is isolation. It was good that they asked a question. Often there are officers that genuinely care, and when I hear that I feel good that there is an officer that gets it, but many are just doing it as part of their duty. The way the system is set up is that most of the time we connect with our clients through the police. They are the first point of contact."

"I've always wanted to provide a service to the community. Growing up in the Native American community, I felt like it was my duty to give back to the community. I wanted to be a resource to someone and help prevent and intervene when there were issues because the violence flows down to their children. Someone is stationed at the police station to answer calls and to follow up on cases. It is not their area of expertise, so having advocates available to provide insight or assistance is very

helpful. There is a lot of mistrust with the community and the police. The relationship is strained and there is a lot of uncertainty with making police calls."

"Well, twice during a meal, they came downstairs. Yeah. And that just creates chaos. It's really hard to deal with when it happens. Cause, like, it makes everybody feel uneasy. And it actually makes people scatter. Like, people actually leave the space. I mean people will actually physically scatter. Like they will leave the building, they will go outdoors, they don't ever go in or out. Like, um, folks will hide. And they'll leave. And then, when you're trying to create community, it's heartbreaking. And then, we'll be quiet that whole week, cause people just don't show up. Cause the words gets out real quick that the cops were there on Monday, and everyone assumes they're looking for them, even though they actually are not. A lot of my folks do have outstanding warrants and stuff like that. But even the folks who don't, scatter. And they don't feel safe. And folks who are former felons, and folks who are still on paper, and they just don't...if the police are in that space, especially if they're in uniform, and they're...it's no longer a safe space for them."

"Queer and trans youth with whom we work, especially queer trans youth of color, have said time and time again that where they experience the most violence is with the police."

"A lot of the time they're [the police] just staying in their cars and just getting out when something bad happens. Literally doing no prevention of any kind, and if the community felt like they actually cared about the safety of the community and not just, like bad guys vs. good guys, whatever dynamic ends up happening, I think that it would impact crime rates completely. But the way that they often do it, and the way that the system is set up, is like fear tactics, patrolling from their cars with their tinted windows and we're already afraid of shit going down in the neighborhood...they're not making it safer, they're making it worse, you know?"

"I don't use that world as a resource for support or safety. Only use as a last resort. Maybe I have called [the police] twice in twenty-five years. I work with an organization where we do have to partner with the police. The kids we work with feel the most unsafe with the police. Hosts also know that most of the young people do not want to interface with the police."

"Feeling like the police are not really helpful. We often have to use the police to take someone to the hospital for mental health, etc. It feels more like a taxi ride versus a service. It's often written all over their body language that they don't want to be here, it's not a priority for them, it's written all over their body language which is why it's better to call someone who is trained to look at the situation for what it is. This is a person having a mental health crisis, the proper response is to address the person's mental health. They are not trying to see the truth of what is happening, they are going through the motions, getting the bullet points, collecting the reports."

"What we see is that homeless youth... we see that the white kids get funneled into mental health facilities and POC kids get funneled into the criminal justice system, which sets them up to have a record which makes it very difficult for them to get a job."

"I had a client who had been raped at the Metro Transit station, she was lured into a parking garage and raped. So she was really proactive [...] So her reaction was 'Okay, I'mma go to the police, I'mma make a police report, I'mma go to the emergency room, get checked out, and then I'm gonna go make an appointment with my therapist.' She had, like, she knew what she needed to do [...] And I took her to the police station to make a police report. And the officer who was there, that just happened to be his beat. He was familiar—that's his route, this parking garage is on his route. He's familiar with that area. So he was coming from a place of 'We're gonna get this guy,' he wanted to help her, it was good, but he was [...] almost parental about it. He was like, 'Well, why were you there so late at night?' Yeah, he didn't say, 'What were you wearing,' which is the classic line, but he said EVERYTHING else. 'Why were you there so late at night? Why didn't you have a friend? Why are you taking the bus to work so early in the morning? Why don't you take an Uber?'[...] I had to keep telling him, I had to keep bringing him back, he's like 'Well why did you do this, why did you do this,' instead of saying, 'Where did you get raped, what time, what did the person look like, what did he do after,' that kinda interview. He was focused just, like, entirely on her behavior, not on this person. So I felt like I was running the interview. And this guy was in his fifties. I was like, 'Dude, how long have you been doing this for? I just happened to sit in on your making a report for a sexual assault, and you are doing it all wrong.' He was like, 'Well I've had training, and I know where you're coming from, and I'm not trying to yell at you, but if my daughter got into this situation [...]' 'Cause he has kids, right? Father figure. I was so proud of her, she's like 'Well I'm

not your fucking daughter? Right? Am I? No? I need help. Quit scolding me and get the information.'[...] So, you know, I haven't heard from him since, I see him every once in awhile, but, man. If I could just sit him down for a few hours and let him know what he's doing wrong in a way that's professional, I wish. I wish. But he's not forced to do that for me, or for anyone else."

"It's like what was y'all doing? If y'all are so present, why aren't y'all really present? They're all out here, but what are y'all really doing? Like I said, it makes people look at police like, "Why are y'all here if y'all not going to really serve or protect how y'all are supposed to? Serving and protecting, it shouldn't be something that's optional."

"There are a lot of male clients coming in that feel like they wouldn't be believed by the police that they are being abused because they should be this strong black man or that they might be viewed as the aggressor."

"The police do not treat men or gender nonconforming people in the same way (as they treat women). When they do call police, it sometimes takes two hours for the police to arrive after a domestic violence call is made. By the time the police do come, the perpetrator might be gone and it's really hard on the victim and it discourages them to call. It is not always effective."

"When a victim acts in self-defense, often the victim will get arrested. It's often difficult for the police to pinpoint the primary aggressor, especially in same-sex relationships."

"When confronted with evidence of police terror, the government responds with public relations campaigns."

MPD ESCALATES RATHER THAN DE-ESCALATES:

MPD RESPONSE TO CRISES DOESN'T REDUCE HARM; IT AMPLIFIES HARM

"I've had a conversation with my director of security, so I can speak to the conversation he and I have, more than I can talk about with my other two guys, but the conversation that he and I have is that we don't call the cops if we can help it. Because we don't trust that they're gonna show up in a way that actually de-escalates the situation, where it would be good for us. With relationship to our guests and clients that we love."

"We need the police to act a little more like a social worker and less like a soldier."

"If you are the victim of a crime...and there might be chemical dependency stuff involved, there might be mental health stuff involved too, but if the core of it is you're the victim of a crime, I still want you to have you agency and have your power. And that gets taken away when cops show up too. That somehow then you're just supposed to hand all this over to them, and they're gonna solve it and fix it, and bring some form of justice. And since generally, that's not my experience of how it works? It's not working."

"So when they see the homeless shelter, they're automatically thinking 'this person's violent, dangerous, we need to get them out right away.' They're just—anger, frustration, confusion. It's a really delicate situation to deal with. I've had to personally throw myself in front of a cop before because they were acting way too aggressively for the situation for my client."

"When you see the cops you're always on your guard. You think they could be coming for me, or something easily could have set them off. Something small I do might be able to set them off. If I have my hands in my pocket, or if I'm reaching for my wallet, if I'm checking my timer or watch. Just being conscious of any kind of action, any small action, could have a drastic impact or it could be the last thing I do. Yeah, just always being just still like a statue. I can't be myself around cops or anything."

"Just the whole profiling aspect of it is terrible, getting pulled over just because you look like another African-American male or nothing like an African-American male or whatever. Yeah, I mean it just makes you be more cautious. I'm always cautious when I'm driving. I'm cautious when I'm out and about in public outside of my door. Have to always be conscious of the fact that I'm Black and I can be easily profiled, easily targeted. I have to always walk with that in the forefront of my mind no matter where I am...You should feel safe, but you feel on your guard."

"We work with the police all of the time. Nine out of ten people are never going to report to the police ever. They might be going to the hospital for the sexual assault exam but they are not making a police report [...] Sexual assault is a tool of oppression and it is disproportionately felt by marginalized communities [...] A lot of people who are sexually assaulted have a history with police already, and that history is one where the police were agents of violence against them. So it wouldn't occur to them to turn to the police when violence has happened to them, because the police are not safe people to them and they never have been. The police are agents of violence to them. We work with how to improve the support victims receive after sexual assault [...] it's hard on our part to move people forward after they have experienced sexual violence because the path that is available to victims is not a healthy, safe, and restorative path [...] there is tremendous pressure on Black women to not send another Black man to jail. They are really discouraged in the community from reporting at all or reaching out for service."

"The police ain't never helped me in my life. They've always hindered me in some type of way. Actually, I really thought that when me and you had got into it if the police would have came in time it wouldn't have been a problem, but they came super late and they was super aggressive. It was too much. They've never been there when they needed to be for me. They always there when it's time for me to be in trouble. Not when I need them."

"We had called 911 for medical help—the EMT took care of it and the police came and were very forceful and were trying to force their way into the shelter even though we were clear that we didn't need them anymore. The situation had been taken

care of and they didn't believe me and they were kind of confrontational and pushing and I wouldn't let them in the building because there was no reason for them to be in the building."

"Staff at [name of org. omitted] are really good about letting youth know, police are coming, if you need to leave you should. We know that most of the kids we work with are not comfortable with police around. That's where they live, it is their home and most of them don't have anything positive to say about the police, they do not want to see them."

IT IS DANGEROUS TO CALL UPON, TALK, INTERACT, OR COLLABORATE WITH MPD:
"9-1-1'S A JOKE IN YOUR TOWN"

"They rarely have the response we are hoping for—they are not interested in really helping people in the way that they need it. This population of people are not a priority for them, their responses are often robotic. They are not really trying to see the 'truth' of what is happening. It's better for us to call someone that is trained to look at the situation globally."

"I want to say, when's the last time you had a mental health training? When's the last time you interacted with a trans client? When's the last time you've sat with someone and talked with them about their sex trafficking experience? You know, like, I'm seeing that there's not a lot of training in your field, and there's plenty of training in mine, so guess what? Imma go with what I know. Enough to tell my clients what I know. It's as simple as that. I'm not trying to make them hate the cops, I'm not trying to enforce this "don't trust the police" mentality, but it's like, simply you have other options. Unless someone's trying to kill you. Which, I mean, a lot of times it is that kinda situation, in which case, when is it good to call the cops, when is it bad to call the cops? So, that's kinda where I'm at."

"Then another experience was I was pregnant [...] and I was at [a] memorial block party. Some stuff happened, an altercation with a couple people [...]

I was walking past with my two girl cousins on the side of me because I had just fell but they held me up because when all the commotion was going on I was trying to get out the way. They held me up. I was walking across the street and then we were going to the police to tell them what happened. Then they maced all three of us. That night I had to spend the night in the hospital because of that, because I swallowed mace and everything."

"We've had a couple instances where police have arrested victim-survivors with warrants."

"Once I was coming back from a party and everything was good. For once there was no fighting and no shooting after a party. It was so good. Then the police came and it was like me and seven other people standing on this gate that was in the alley. The police, we seen them riding through the alley where we were standing, but we thought they were just about to go past because we weren't doing nothing to anyone, no fights or nothing. Next thing you know they stop right at the beginning of the line of us. I was kind of in the middle. They stopped and next thing you know he started driving real fast. He rolled the window down and just maced all of us in a line."

MPD IS BEYOND REFORM:
SLAPPING PAINT ON A HOUSE WITH A BAD FOUNDATION IS FUTILE

"I actually got in a full-blown argument at—what was it? It was a panel discussion; I was with the chief of police's assistant for Hennepin County, I was with an FBI agent, and also with a—it was the worst panel I've ever been on. Um, it was a public defender, but not the good kind. And it was me [...] my policy is to train or give my clients the skills to use their community instead of the police. What can you do? [...] Ooh man, the people on our panel did not like that information. They're like, 'What? What do you mean you're telling your clients not to call the cops?' They have trauma! I'm not gonna force them to call the cops! It's as simple as that!"

"There was a retired, a retired police officer... He's the only one I ever liked. Um, but it was interesting. He was like, because he was retired, he had a lot more freedom to say what he wanted to say [...] and he was like, when you work with police, like, one of the things he said that stuck with me, he was like, when you work with police, be mindful that a lot of them are shitheads. Like, a lot of them are not for their better interests, like a lot of them are like, because they like power and because they have a paycheck. He's like, you have to find a specific person and connect with that person all of the time because most of them are not that way. Like it really hit me, because I was like this is like this old, he was like a seventy-year-old white dude, and like he was like, yup. Police are fucked up. Like, they go, they do a lot of shit, and like, I, he was in leadership at the time. And he was like, even when you're in leadership you can't say anything. Because if you say something that's your job on the line."

Interviewer: "Okay. What would good policing look like, if at all?"

Respondent: "Hmm. I don't know. I mean, maybe the old school image of the cop on their beat. Like, the one cop walking. Talking to... they're a part of the neighborhood. They know families. They know your grandmother. They're just kind of kicking it. Walking around. I feel like the image of that in my mind is attractive, but at this point I don't know if we could make that happen. If we could go back to that place. Or really, if communities of predominantly Black people consistently have ever experienced that."

"I don't think they're bad people in general, not all of them, but I do think that they were never designed to help us in any place that does things without us, plans things without us, is not about us."

"With the police here I think it just has a negative impact because, I don't know, I think we're just kind of used to it by now, Black people because... I think it's just this long-instilled mental trauma that's

happened since the beginning... and it's just migrated until today with police and brutality. Just even starting with slavery, starting way back, just that whole abuse and trauma of slavery and how it's just shifted from that to civil rights to today even with the Black president... all this time people, Black people, has been oppressed. It's just changed. Those forms of oppression, forms of abuse have just shifted. Oppression has changed in its form since time, but it's still there and just as harmful."

"Once a month I sit in a meeting where there are cops there. Advocates from legal, advocacy, health, and law enforcement. Sometimes it is helpful but sometimes it is not. The people that are there really want to change the system to help improve responses to people who experience sexual violence, but I personally don't believe that the policing system can be changed. So it's challenging to work with, even when the individuals are good people that are there. Sometimes I feel like I am working toward something that I don't really believe in."

~~~

ABOLITION, NOT REFORM, IS THE WAY FORWARD

Community interviews on how MPD functions show *why* MPD would need to hire a marketing firm to convince the community that they exist to serve and protect rather than terrorize. When it comes to the notion of police reform, an emphasis is placed on the *appearance* of legitimate authority and fairness where none exists. According to the first of six pillars presented in the presidential report by the Department of Justice on 21st century policing, "People are more likely to obey the law when they believe that those who are enforcing it [cops] have the legitimate authority to tell them what to do."[6]

The attempt, or at least the perceived attempt, to diversify a police force to include more non-white officers is a

[6]   President's Task Force on 21st Century Policing. Final Report of the President's Task Force on 21st Century Policing. Washington, DC: Office of Community Oriented Policing Services. 2015.

common but ineffective response to the community demands to address police terror. One such example of this played out recently in 2017 when the former chief of MPD was forced to resign directly following the shooting of Justine Damond, an affluent white woman, by a Black Somali-American officer. The mayor immediately appointed a new Black chief of police. Data shows that hiring more non-white officers does not reduce police violence.[7] Neither does hiring more women officers, who are more likely to shoot than their male counterparts. The primary correlation of an increase in shootings by police is not an increase in crime, but simply an increase in Black residents.[8,9]

In 2016, a group of researchers at the University of Cincinnati analyzed sixty studies on the relationship between numbers of police and crime levels from 1968 to 2013. The data showed that increasing the numbers of police does not reduce crime, and reducing the numbers of police doesn't increase crime. One of the researchers stated, "...We can reduce police staffing some amount and use that money to renovate our neighborhoods and our communities. And I think that's better than just increasing the police force."[10]

Promises to reform MPD through culture and policy changes are not new, but they are futile. Trying to reform MPD makes about as much sense as trying to reform, rather than abolish, the institution of slavery in the 1800s. Countless individuals, as well as formal and informal collective efforts, planted seeds that, over time, sprouted into the growth of that abolitionist movement.

The notion of not only *envisioning* a Minneapolis without police but actively *working toward* a police-free society is not as outlandish as some may initially think. In fact, when Minneapolis mayoral and city council candidates

Photo by Annabelle Marcovici

"The apologists for slavery often speak of the abuses of slavery; and they tell us that they are as much opposed to those abuses as we are; and that they would go as far to correct those abuses and to ameliorate the condition of the slave as anybody. The answer to that view is that slavery is itself an abuse; that it lives by abuse, and dies by the lack of abuse."

-Frederick Douglass, The Prospect in the Future, August 1860

for 2017 were asked if they believe that "we could ever have a city without police," nine candidates responded in the affirmative. One candidate replied, "I can imagine that world, and I think that's the world I want to live in." These responses were published by Voices for Racial Justice and Pollen in a non-partisan voter guide.[11,12,13,14]

A look at the past and the present has established that the institution of policing cannot be reformed, and as a community, our resources should be used to work toward abolishing it. The time to divest in the Minneapolis Police Department is now. The time to invest in community-based safety programs is now.

Abolition is the only way forward.

7 Bouie, Jamelle. "Why More Diverse Police Departments Won't Put an End to Police Misconduct ." Slate Magazine. October 13, 2014. Accessed November 14, 2017. http://www.slate.com/articles/news_and_politics/politics/2014/10/diversity_won_t_solve_police_misconduct_black_cops_don_t_reduce_violence.html.

8 Ibid.

9 Smith, Brad W. "The Impact of Police Officer Diversity on Police-Caused Homicides." Policy Studies Journal 31, no. 2 (2003): 147-62. doi:10.1111/1541-0072.t01-1-00009.

10 Lee, Yongjei, John E. Eck, and Nicholas Corsaro. "Conclusions from the history of research into the effects of police force size on crime—1968 through 2013: a historical systematic review." Journal of Experimental Criminology 12, no. 3 (2016): 431-51. doi:10.1007/s11292-016-9269-8.

11 Smith, Brad W. "The Impact of Police Officer Diversity on Police-Caused Homicides." Policy Studies Journal 31, no. 2 (2003): 147-62. doi:10.1111/1541-0072.t01-1-00009.

12 Bouie, Jamelle. "Why More Diverse Police Departments Won't Put an End to Police Misconduct ." Slate Magazine. October 13, 2014. Accessed November 14, 2017. http://www.slate.com/articles/news_and_politics/politics/2014/10/diversity_won_t_solve_police_misconduct_black_cops_don_t_reduce_violence.html.

13 "Voter Guide." Pollen. Accessed November 14, 2017. https://www.pollenmidwest.org/voter-guide/.

14 Belz, Adam. "Some Minneapolis candidates say they can envision a city without police." Star Tribune. October 5, 2017. Accessed November 14, 2017. http://www.startribune.com/some-city-council-candidates-say-they-can-envision-a-minneapolis-without-police/449500303/.

A COMMUNITY CENTERED LIFESTYLE WHERE THE YOUNG, OLD & EVERYONE IN BETWEEN ARE FULL PARTICIPANTS. EVERYONE'S WHOLE PERSONHOOD IS PRIORITIZED.

WE ARE COMMITTED EVERYONE' NEEDS BEING WE BELIEVE SOLUTIONS ARE BIG EN TO EMBRA US AL

PEOPLE TAKE OWNERSHIP OF PUBLIC SPACES AND RESPECT BOUNDARIES & COLLECTIVITY. WE HAVE HARD CONVERSATIONS WITH OURSELVES & EACH OTHER. WE MAKE ROOM FOR LAUGHTER.

REE world look like?*

BY TORI HONG

WE PROTECT EACH OTHER. PEOPLE HAVE MORE CAPACITY TO BUILD, DREAM & IMAGINE. WE CAN FOCUS ON HEALING HISTORICAL AND INTER-GENERATIONAL TRAUMA.

JUSTICE IS PRIORITIZED OVER RETRIBUTION. HEALING IS PRIORITIZED OVER RIGHTEOUSNESS. NO ONE IS DISPOSABLE.

THE COMMUNITY GETS TO BELIEVE IN ITS OWN POWER AGAIN. WE HAVE THE ANSWERS TO HEAL & KEEP EACH OTHER SAFE, WE JUST NEED THE SPACE TO DO IT.

An example of a resource sheet made in Minneapolis circa 2019. Putting together a one-sheet like this, and sharing it with neighbors or friends, can be a relatively quick, immediately useful project for members of other communities looking to spread the word about non-police resources to call upon.

MINNEAPOLIS & HENNEPIN COUNTY
RESOURCES LIST

SOCIAL SERVICES

United Way 2-1-1 provides free and confidential health and human services information for people in Minnesota. Available 24/7 for crisis and non-emergency situations.

The Sexual Violence Center supports everyone affected by sexual violence. 24-hour crisis line: 612-871-5111

Tubman provides family violence safety planning. 24-hour crisis and resource line: 612-825-0000.

Minnesota Warmline provides a safe, anonymous and confidential phone and text service for people working on their mental health recovery. Call Mon-Sat, 5-10 PM: 651-288-0400 or text "Support" to 85511

St. Stephen's provides street outreach, shelter, and supportive housing. More info online: ststephensmpls.org

ADDITIONAL RESOURCES

Narcan (noloxone) is a medication used to stop heroin or other opiate overdose. Anyone can get Narcan without a prescription at **Red Door** for themselves, friends or family members: Health Services Building, 525 Portland Ave, 4th Floor in downtown Minneapolis; 612-543-5555.

MN Poison Control System Call 1-800-222-1222 for all poison emergencies and questions. Poison experts are available 24/7.

Minneapolis 311 provides information about City services (need to report a pothole? lost cat? etc.) Call 311 or 612-673-3000.

MENTAL HEALTH EMERGENCY

Mobile crisis teams*
Adults, 18 and older:
COPE – 612-596-1223

Children, ages 17 and younger:
Child Crisis – 612-348-2233

*they may choose to send police

Crisis Text Line free help across the state; text MN to 741 741

Trans Lifeline: anonymous and confidential. If in crisis, they will not call police unless you want them to: 877-565-8860

National Suicide Hotline: 24/7, free and confidential support for people in distress, prevention and crisis resources for you or your loved ones: 1-800-273-8255

PLANTING THE SEEDS OF ABOLITION

What are other ways we can imagine a police-free world? What actions can we take now, to build this future?

- **Get to know and talk to your neighbors**. Reach out to a trusted community member.
- **Take a first aid and/or CPR class.** Check out Minneapolis Community Education or the YWCA for low-cost options.
- **Pods and pod-mapping worksheet:** who are the pods of people you would call on if you've been harmed, caused harm, or witnessed harm? More at bit.ly/PodsResource
- Learn more about **transformative justice** at TransformHarm.org, a resource hub about ending violence.

Where We're Going:
Alternatives in the Making

Introduction

In the first section of this report, we reviewed the corrupt, brutal, and oppressive history of the Minneapolis Police Department. In the second section, we discussed the current landscape of the community-police relationship in Minneapolis. In this final section, we will present our thoughts on some ways we could bring this 150-year-long tragedy to its close and begin a new chapter in the history of Minneapolis.

We've explored the problems deep in the heart of our police department. The culture of MPD is one where racism and brutality are tacitly allowed, and officers are honor-bound to cover up for one another's misconduct. Complaints of officer misconduct are dismissed, covered up, and ignored, and even when officers are found guilty of brutality, the city can't hold them accountable, and many of them continue to work on the force. Community outrage leads to cries for civilian review, diversity training, and body cameras—all of which ultimately fail to address the underlying problems. Meanwhile, the police union has a formidable amount of political power, and they use that power to prevent, limit, and destroy even small attempts at accountability. 150 years of history shows us that police reform is impossible: it's time to dream bigger. It's time to dream of police abolition.

Imagine for a moment that you were asked to help create stability in a newly founded city that includes a healthy and safe environment. How would you try to solve the problems that your friends and neighbors encountered? How would you respond to crisis and violence? Would your first choice be an unaccountable army with a history of oppression and violence patrolling your neighborhood around the clock?

To begin envisioning a different world, we have to start by breaking down the functions that police hold in our communities. Right now, police are tasked with three major things in our city: they maintain order, respond to crisis, and bring criminals to "justice."

Maintaining Order

Our criminal justice system is built on the idea that crime is a form of individual misbehavior, and can be prevented by putting "bad guys" in jail. On the other hand, common sense and social sciences research tell us that most crime is caused by poverty and marginalization, and cannot be prevented without addressing the underlying causes. In the words of retired Minneapolis Police Chief Tony Bouza, "The idea of police as crime preventers is rubbish. By the time the cop appears, the criminal has been formed and the crime has been committed."[1]

When human beings lived in smaller communities where most people knew each other, crime wasn't nearly as much of a concern as it is now. These days, we live in massive communities where a few people control most of the wealth and power, and the rest of us have to get by on scraps. Of course there's crime and disorder in our city, given our state, our country, and our world. But the solution to that crime and disorder isn't locking people up—it's making sure they have what they need to get by. As Greg Boyle, founder of Homeboy Industries, a community safety agency in Los Angeles put it, "nothing stops a bullet like a job."[2] Giving our communities the resources they need to thrive will do far more to prevent theft, assault, and murder than "tough on crime" policing ever could.

But stopping crime isn't even what dominates the time of police officers—parking tickets and traffic stops take up far more of most officers' time. It's 2017—there are far better ways to give someone a speeding ticket than having someone with a gun pull you over on the highway, putting both of your lives at risk. Let's find ways of holding each other accountable for harm in ways that don't require the threat of violence.

In addition to "preventing crime," police also enforce the morality of the powerful on everyone else. This means forcing unhoused people out of sight, criminalizing drug users, and incarcerating sex workers, even when their choices don't harm anyone. Centuries of criminalization haven't ended homelessness, drug use, or sex work—it's time to reexamine our relationship with what the rich and powerful deem "unacceptable."

Finally, maintaining order requires that any challenge to authority is brutally crushed—this was as true during the 1934 Truckers' Strike, as it was during the 1999 Minnehaha Free State, as it was in the aftermath of the murder of Jamar Clark in 2015. As long as we have a militarized police force ready to attack anyone who threatens the status quo, advocates for social justice will suffer violence, imprisonment, and the difficulty of finding a job and housing with a criminal record. Is that really how we want our community to respond to calls for us to treat each other better?

---

1   Anthony V. Bouza, Police Unbound: Corruption, Abuse, and Heroism by the Boys in Blue (Amherst, NY: Prometheus Books, 2001). Pg. 140.
2   Nico Pitney, "Nothing Stops A Bullet Like A Job," The Huffington Post, September 30, 2015. Accessed November 05, 2017. https://www.huffingtonpost.com/entry/greg-boyle-homeboy-industries-life-lessons_us_56030036e4b00310edf9c7a4.

Responding to Crisis

When someone makes a 9-1-1 call, the police are almost always dispatched, even in cases that primarily concern paramedics or firefighters. Police are poorly trained to deal with the vast majority of crises; for every call in which the use of violence becomes necessary, there are many mental health crises and domestic violence calls that cops are poorly equipped to deal with. The solution isn't trying to train officers to do everything—it's a more specialized and decentralized response to emergencies.

9-1-1 didn't exist until the 1980s in Minnesota. At the time, plenty of people were skeptical of the idea of dispatching police, paramedics, and firefighters from the same call, given the different functions they serve. But if dispatchers can decide which of those three services to dispatch to an emergency, why not more? Why not have mental health professionals, social workers, domestic violence advocates, and other responders who could be dispatched to the scene depending on the situation? Or, to put it differently, how many 9-1-1 calls actually require the involvement of people with guns?

Criminal Justice

When's the last time you heard of someone in your life reporting a theft to the police? Was the perpetrator caught? Did the victim get their property back? How about the last time you heard of someone being held accountable for a sexual assault after the survivor reported it to the police? The fact of the matter is that police aren't that good at solving crimes, even ones as serious as murder. For example, in 2015, MPD only solved 26 out of the 45 murders that were committed.[3] Part of the problem is a lack of trust in the police—many residents don't report crimes in the first place, or refuse to provide evidence based on past experiences with the police. To try to get around these issues, MPD invests in programs to get witnesses to talk to police, including a group of community leaders who provide counseling after shootings and a team of social workers at Hennepin County Medical Center who try to discourage retaliatory violence. But if we want to be able to address violence and harm in constructive ways, leaving crime investigation in the hands of a largely mistrusted agency overly reliant on incarceration is not an option, regardless of their outreach efforts.

Other models can help us learn how to respond to harm in ways that allow for humanity and growth on the part of the victim and the perpetrator. These can include traditional methods of peace-making practiced by peoples around the world, as well as more immediate options: for example, restorative justice agencies here in the Twin Cities that currently work in the criminal justice system could be tasked with addressing community conflict outside of the courtroom. Another model to consider is the Truth and Reconciliation Commission that helped South Africa begin to heal from the wounds of apartheid. One thing is certainly true: we couldn't design a more inhumane, racist, damaging way to resolve conflict than the United States penal system if we tried.

Investing in a Better Future

We can live in safe and healthy communities without police; in fact, the criminalization and violence police bring into our communities make them even less safe. What we need are resources—the time and support to build a network of community safety providers that don't solve every difficult problem with the threat of force. The mayor's proposed

[3] Jany, Libor. "More killings go unsolved in Minneapolis." Star Tribune (Minneapolis), October 16, 2016.

budget for 2018 increases the funding of the Minneapolis Police Department to $179.2 million a year. Think about what that money could do if it were used to help people out of poverty, build affordable housing, or invest in jobs programs, education, addiction treatment, mental health services, and beyond. 150 years of investing in the Minneapolis Police Department certainly hasn't ended harm in our city—it's time we tried something new.

Divestment doesn't have to happen overnight. We can take our time building the alternatives that we need to keep our communities safe, pulling a few dollars at a time out of the police budget and putting them into other community safety options. Right now is a good time to start—"Baby Boomer" police officers are retiring in large numbers, and departments across the country are struggling to replace them. One potential road to divestment could begin with a hiring freeze—as each Baby Boomer police officer retires, their salary gets transferred into a new community safety program.

These ideas aren't just utopian dreams—support for police abolition is growing across the country. Activists in Chicago, New York, Durham, and other cities are advocating for "Beyond Policing" platforms that ask city officials to redirect police budgets into community-led safety initiatives. The idea of investing in police alternatives has already been tested in Minneapolis: in 2016, the City Council voted to invest $500,000 into community-led safety programs in the Broadway and Little Earth communities. But half a million dollars is a drop in the bucket compared to the hundreds of millions we spend on the police every year. If we really want to build a safer and more humane future, we'll need to dream a lot bigger.

The first step on the road to a police-free city is determining the needs of our communities, and identifying alternatives that can meet those needs.

MPD150 doesn't claim to have all the answers, but we do know that given a chance, our communities will rise to the occasion of creating a better world for our children.

Who You Gonna Call?

We don't have the resources we need to begin living in a police-free city tomorrow, but we do have what we need to get started. In the next few pages, we'll share some ideas about how to use existing programs to begin building out a community safety network that can replace the police. If any of these resources sound like they would be helpful to you, you can find out more about them, including contact information, on our website at www.mpd150.com. We'll begin by looking at one of the duties that police are least well-equipped to deal with: responding to calls where someone is having a mental health crisis.

Mental Health Crisis Response

It's no secret that the United States doesn't have adequate mental health care facilities. Ever since most mental hospitals were defunded and closed down in the 1960s and 1970s, there has been little recourse for people going through psychological crises. Right now, when someone experiencing a crisis calls 911, the police are the first people dispatched. It's estimated that one in ten police calls involves someone experiencing a mental health crisis, but police are poorly trained to deal with those crises.

In the United States, the average police officer receives fifty-eight hours of firearms training and forty-nine hours of defensive tactical training, but only eight hours of descalation training, a key element of helping to resolve mental health crises.[4] In Minneapolis, police officers go through forty hours of Crisis Intervention Training designed to help them deal with these situations,

and the department is starting to train mental health co-responders, but the fact remains that police departments are still poorly equipped to deal with mental health crises when compared to community healers and mental health professionals. This reality is reflected in the long history, both in Minneapolis and around the country, of people with mental illness being brutalized and killed by police officers.

Thankfully, we already have a number of alternatives to the police in dealing with mental health crises in Minneapolis. Hennepin County has a program called COPE (Community Outreach for Psychiatric Services) that will dispatch qualified mental health responders to your location at any time of the day or night. There's a similar program for responding to youth mental health crises called Hennepin County Child Crisis, too. We also have a network of locally-based mental health crisis hotlines like Crisis Connection, Tubman's Crisis Line, and MN Warmline.

The biggest limitation that mental health crisis response programs face is a lack of resources. If we funded mental health care services more broadly in our society, there wouldn't be as many crises to begin with. Even the programs we have go underfunded: Crisis Connection, which has operated for nearly fifty years, was nearly shut down in the summer of 2017 after state legislators refused to set aside $1.4 million to continue funding it.[5] COPE doesn't get enough money either—when all of their responders are already dispatched and they receive a call, all they can do is tell the person requesting help to call the police department. If we want our city to care for people experiencing mental health crises, we should make mental health responders our first responders, rather than an afterthought.

Homelessness

Ever since Minnesota passed its first vagrancy law in the early 1900s, one of the duties of the Minneapolis Police

4   Lyden, Tom. "Twin Cities officers taking Crisis Intervention Training to help people with mental illness." Fox 9. November 21, 2016. Accessed November 14, 2017. http://www.fox9.com/news/i investigators/investigators-a-softer-shade-of-blue.

5   Sepic, Matt. "Crisis Connection hotline rescued, at least temporarily." Minnesota Public Radio News. July 14, 2017. Accessed November 14, 2017. https://www.mprnews.org/story/2017/07/14/crisis-connection-hotline-rescued-at-least-temporarily.

Department has been to round up and criminalize people experiencing homelessness. That remains true today; Minneapolis has criminalized a range of activities that are unavoidable for many homeless folks, including begging in some places, sleeping in vehicles, and using temporary structures such as tents.[6] Police come into contact with people experiencing homelessness in other ways, too: when people fearful of those without housing call 911, or when police are tasked with "cleaning up" an area of the city prior to a major event like the Super Bowl. Arresting, brutalizing, and criminalizing people experiencing homelessness doesn't help them to find stable housing; in fact, it makes it more difficult for them to do so. We need to find better ways of dealing with our housing problems.

Some of the resources we need to solve our housing crisis already exist: Minneapolis has a number of shelters and social service providers that can help people experiencing homelessness find a place to sleep, short or long term. We have a particularly strong network of resources for youth experiencing homelessness, including organizations like Streetworks, Avenues for Homeless Youth, The Bridge, and Youthlink. There's even a street outreach team run by St. Stephens that seeks to be the first point of contact for people living on the street, helping to provide them with resources and sometimes intervening in community-police interactions that would otherwise lead to arrest.[7]

We have an affordable housing crisis in Minneapolis. The vacancy rate for rentals hovers around 2%, and the population is growing rapidly without building enough new housing.[8] Meanwhile, our homeless shelters are filled to capacity: we only have around 600 beds for single adults in the city, and dozens of people are turned away every night, forced to sleep outside because of a lack of funding.[9] If we want to solve homelessness in Minneapolis, we should start there—by increasing the number of shelter beds available, building

more affordable housing, and resisting gentrification—not by asking police to arrest our way out of the problem.

Traffic Stops

One of the common things police officers do are "suspicious person," "suspicious vehicle," and "traffic law enforcement" stops. People of color are disproportionately pulled over in these stops on flimsy pretexts, sometimes being searched with the hopes that police will turn up evidence of criminal activity. An ACLU report from 2015 found that people of color are far more likely to be arrested for normal traffic violations—for example, Black people were almost nine times as likely as white people to be arrested when pulled over in the middle of the day.

Traffic stops aren't just minor annoyances; they're dangerous, for both community members and officers. Philando Castile was killed during a traffic stop after being pulled over 49 times in 13 years, and although it's rare for police officers to be shot while on duty, many of the shootings that do happen occur during traffic stops.

Traffic stops don't make sense as a community safety practice. What little good they do is outweighed by the harassment and violence they inflict on marginalized communities. Those that investigate "suspicious" people or vehicles should be eliminated entirely: no one should have to be harassed or searched by the police just because of their appearance. There are better ways we could handle traffic violations, too: if someone has a broken tail light, for example, a warning in the mail would not only be as effective as a traffic stop, but a safer way to let them know.

Many states already do this with toll violations. Even with more immediate violations, like speeding or reckless driving, bringing an armed police officer into the situation just makes it more

likely that the stop will end in tragedy. Traffic stops are a bad idea, and we should look to other ways to keep our streets safe.

Domestic Violence

What do you do when you're in a relationship that turns violent? People experiencing domestic violence may need someone to step in, may need a safe place to go, may need a loved one to leave, and may need emotional support. Calling the police means they will be met with violent force in a situation where they are already facing violence. They may be putting a loved one's life in danger, as well as their own life. Police officers are also two to four times more likely to *commit* domestic violence than other community members, making them a poor choice for survivors seeking help.[10]

Minneapolis has a number of existing resources for people experiencing domestic violence including stalking, verbal, emotional, and physical abuse. The Tubman Crisis Line, Crisis Connection, Sexual Violence Center, Cornerstone, MN Day One Crisis Hotline, OutFront and Advocare have crisis hotlines. The Domestic Abuse Project has a crisis hotline during business hours on weekdays, individual and group counseling for adults and children experiencing abuse, as well as support for adults who have committed abuse and are working to stop the cycle of abuse. Crisis Connection in Washington and Anoka Counties create mobile crisis response teams that respond to calls when appropriate.

People experiencing domestic violence need to establish personal safety for themselves and other family members affected by the violence. Having trusted community members available to respond to violent situations is a necessity. Those who respond need to be able to read the situation and be prepared to intervene, de-escalate, and/

6   National Law Center on Homelessness & Poverty. Housing Not Handcuffs: Ending the Criminalization of Homelessness in U.S. Cities. 2016.
7   "Street Outreach." St. Stephen's Human Services. October 24, 2017. Accessed November 14, 2017. https://ststephensmpls.org/programs/emergency-shelter/street-outreach.
8   U.S. Department of Housing and Urban Development. Comprehensive Housing Market Analysis as of March 1st, 2017: Minneapolis-St. Paul-Bloomington, Minnesota-Wisconsin. 2017.
9   Furst, Randy. "With too many homeless and too few shelter beds, city funding policy debated." Star Tribune (Minneapolis), September 18, 2017.
10   Friedersdorf, Conor. "Police Have a Much Bigger Domestic-Abuse Problem Than the NFL Does." The Atlantic. September 19, 2014. Accessed November 14, 2017. https://www.theatlantic.com/national/archive/2014/09/police-officers-who-hit-their-wives-or-girlfriends/380329/.

or offer emotional support and access to resources like temporary housing. Those who respond need to prioritize the person experiencing the violence, as well as offer support for the person committing it. Abusers must be held accountable, while prioritizing the needs of victim-survivors, all while following community-determined standards and creating a pathway to healing and reconciliation for the person committing the harm.

Sexual Violence

All violence violates people's boundaries, but sexual violence can be particularly egregious because of the combination of physical, emotional, and sexual boundaries it crosses. As with domestic violence, police are poor responders to sexual violence for a number of reasons, not least of which is that they *commit* sexual violence at rates higher than the general population.[11]

Crisis Connection, RAINN, the Sexual Violence Center, MN Day One Crisis Hotline, and The National Sexual Assault Telephone Hotline all provide hotlines and access to resources. The Stop It Now! Helpline is for adults who are at risk for sexually abusing a child, for friends and family members of sexual assault survivors, and for parents of children with sexual behavior problems.

In addition to what we laid out as necessary responses to domestic violence situations, victim-survivors of sexual assault may need access to specialized physical and emotional support. It is our responsibility as a community to ensure we have people who can provide this support. We also need community members who are ready to engage with the person who committed the sexual assault, to hold them accountable for their actions and address any underlying causes/issues that may have contributed to their actions. We have to prioritize the needs of survivors as well as establish and follow community norms for responding to sexual violence. Find a wealth of writing on abolitionist approaches to preventing sexual violence at our site and at the resource hub TransformHarm.org.

Sex Trafficking and Commercial Sexual Exploitation

Where there is historical trauma, poverty, and economic marginalization, there will always be an opportunity for exploitation. Sex trafficking and commercial sexual exploitation, like other forms of labor trafficking, prey on the vulnerable—those whose agency has been taken away from them by a system that keeps vast numbers of people trapped in a cycle of scarcity—disproportionately women and trans folks from Native communities and communities of color.

There are some resources available now for survivors of trafficking: among others, TeenPRIDE/The Family Partnership serves young women and transgender youth who are survivors of sex trafficking and sex exploitation. Minnesota Indian Women's Sexual Assault Coalition (MIWSAC) and the Minnesota Indian Women's Resource Center (MIWRC) both work specifically within Indigenous communities, providing both direct services and community advocacy. These are only a few organizations among many doing this work, and not to mention the countless individuals who have devoted their time and labor to supporting victim-survivors and ending sex trafficking. On a state level, Minnesota has enacted a No Wrong Doors policy, and became a Safe Harbors State in 2014 (more information available through Minnesota Department of Health). These programs operate from a specific crisis-response lens and have their own shortfalls, but they're a start. While all programming and response efforts continue to evolve, resources still fall short, particularly for adults and families, and marginalized communities are still over-targeted by multiple players and systems.

If we truly want to support survivors, we need to invest in prevention, specifically in ending the economic and social conditions that lead to such deeply rooted vulnerabilities in the first place.

Drug Use

The war on drugs has been very effective in systematically criminalizing communities of color, locking millions of people up, and making billions of dollars for private prison corporations. At the same time, it's been completely ineffective at reducing the availability of drugs or preventing the harm that can come from some drug use.[12] Just as the Minneapolis Police Department failed to stop alcohol consumption during the Prohibition era of the 1920s, they have been unsuccessful at regulating the sale and use of other drugs in the decades since.

Despite the continued criminalization of drug use, there are many resources available in Minneapolis to support users, including counseling, syringe access, HIV testing, and overdose prevention. Some of the organizations and collectives doing this work are H.A.N.D, or Heroin Alternative Needle Distribution, the Minnesota AIDS project, the Minnesota Transgender Health Coalition, and the Morpheus Project.

There's a simple solution to drug use in a police-free world: legalize it. Communities across the United States have been decriminalizing recreational marijuana usage, preventing thousands of community members from being incarcerated for using a relatively harmless drug. Other countries have gone even further: Portugal decriminalized all drugs in 2000, and has seen declines in HIV infection, overdose deaths, and overall drug usage.[13] Of course, decriminalization alone won't undo the harm that the war on drugs has done to communities of color, and any discussion of legalization should include conversations about reparations to communities that have been targeted under the guise of "drug enforcement."

11   Carpenter, Zoë. "The Police Violence We Aren't Talking About." The Nation. June 29, 2015. Accessed November 14, 2017. https://www.thenation.com/article/police-violence-we-arent-talking-about/.

12   Chalabi, Mona. "The 'war on drugs' in numbers: a systematic failure of policy." The Guardian. April 19, 2016. Accessed November 14, 2017. https://www.theguardian.com/world/2016/apr/19/war-on-drugs-statistics-systematic-policy-failure-united-nations.

13   Oakford, Samuel. "Portugal's Example: What Happened After It Decriminalized All Drugs, From Weed to Heroin." VICE News. April 19, 2016. Accessed November 14, 2017. https://news.vice.com/article/ungass-portugal-what-happened-after-decriminalization-drugs-weed-to-heroin.

Sex Work

Despite having existed in Minneapolis since its earliest days, sex work is stigmatized and criminalized in our city. MPD has a long history of extortion and intimidation of sex workers, including cases where police officers lied to sex workers to receive sexual favors, then immediately turned around and arrested them.[14] MPD150 reached out to the Sex Workers Outreach Project Minneapolis (SWOP MPLS) for information on what alternatives are available to the harassment and criminalization they see at the hands of the police. **This is what they sent us:**

"Resources that directly service the sex work community are primarily religious institutions that work in conjunction with law enforcement, ICE, and the anti-trafficking movement. Some organizations operate in a savior modality, and treat all sex work as equal to trafficking.

In terms of non-judgemental resources for sex workers, we mostly have to look to the reproductive rights community, and resources for queer folx. Organizations like Family Tree Clinic, the Aliveness Project, Whole Woman's Health, Red Door Clinic, and Planned Parenthood understand the effect of stigma on sex workers and provide safe spaces for medical care and political support. The Exchange, the Midwest Transgender Health Coalition, and the now defunct MotherShip have provided practical support for the foundation of the Sex Workers Outreach Project MPLS.

SWOP MPLS is the first peer-based organization advocating for the human rights of sex workers in this city. We have collected information on therapists, lawyers, and other service providers who are knowledgeable and sensitive to the needs of sex workers on our website—sadly, this list is not very extensive.

Decriminalization of sex work is the central goal of our movement. Legalization comes with government regulations that will cause new and different harms to sex workers. The way the legal brothels in Nevada and Netherlands operate has proved to be somewhat problematic, and it leaves workers outside of these institutions more vulnerable to legal penalties.[15]

Of course, remaining outside of legalization denies us employee status. Even within sex work that is currently legal, workers are considered independent contractors. The traditional tools for collective bargaining are not available to sex workers. We are trying to envision an independent form of unionizing, where we could use our collective resources to provide ourselves with stuff like insurance, child care, and of course safety precautions. Generally the Sex Workers Rights movement prefers to strengthen independent contractor status rather than advocate to become employees.

There is little recourse, legal or otherwise, for sex workers currently. We have message boards, and other online community spaces where we can report abusive clients to one another. The largest, and most effective board was on Backpage.com, which had its adult entertainment section shut down last winter. Something else will pop up in its place—we are nothing if not resilient—but we need something better. Sex workers tend to have a DIY attitude toward most things in life, and a complicated relationship with capitalism. Most are not revolutionaries, but the community would prefer to be allowed to deal with our issues ourselves."

Property Crime

Most property crime is driven not by malice, but by desperation. A capitalist economy forces each of us to fend for ourselves with little social support or aid. In a time of historically high income inequality, it's no mystery why some people turn to theft, burglary, and other property crime to provide for themselves. The best way to reduce property crime isn't to jail everyone who is poor, or try to scare community members into obedience: it's to invest in communities so that people have less of a need to steal from each other in the first place.

When property crime does occur, oftentimes restorative and transformative justice processes produce better outcomes than arrest and incarceration. In addition to the Native communities who have practiced holistic forms of justice in Minnesota for millennia, we have a number of nonprofits doing restorative justice work in Minneapolis, including Restorative Justice Community Action and Seward Longfellow Restorative Justice Partnership. At present, these agencies work closely with the Minneapolis Police Department and the Hennepin County Court System, allowing for alternative responses to incarceration for minor crimes such as shoplifting, theft, and public urination.

There's no reason, however, that restorative and transformative justice groups can't stand on their own, helping to proactively address conflict in the community without involving the criminal justice system. If we want to reduce property crime, and help heal both perpetrators and victims, we should look to restorative justice rather than police action.

Responding to Violence

We can't discuss how to respond to violence in our communities without acknowledging that police *cause* violence in our communities—directly, through beatings and shootings, and indirectly, through harassment and criminalization.

If we want to end violence in our communities, ending police violence is a necessary step. Police are certainly not the only source of violence in our city. Interpersonal violence has been a

---

14   Collins, Jon. "Mpls. police's prostitution stings criticized." Minnesota Public Radio News. August 20, 2015. Accessed November 14, 2017. https://www.mprnews.org/story/2015/08/20/prostitu
        tion-cop.

15   The World Aids Campaign. Sex Work And the Law: The Case For Decriminalization. Cape Town, South Africa, 2010.

constant throughout human history, and it is only exacerbated by poverty and despair.

Police aren't all that effective at preventing violence. Studies show that increasing or decreasing the number of police officers in a city doesn't affect violent crime levels,[16] and many assaults and murders go unsolved.[17]

What has been shown to be effective are programs that give resources back to the community, empowering us to make our own decisions about how to keep our neighborhoods safe. In the Twin Cities, community efforts to prevent violence include MAD DADs, the Youth Coordinating Board's Outreach Team, and a number of violence prevention initiatives run by the city's Health Department.

Models from elsewhere in the country and the world can provide inspiration as well. Cure Violence's Violence Interruption programs are one example of a program that is empirically proven to be effective at reducing violence.[18] Minneapolis is starting to invest in community-led safety programs, but we have a long way to go if we want to live in a community that deals with violence proactively and humanely.

Responding to violence is one of the most difficult challenges we face as a city, with or without police. But by providing much-needed resources to different communities, giving them space to create their own safety strategies, and reducing our reliance on the ineffective and harmful responses championed by the Minneapolis Police Department, we can create a safer, healthier Minneapolis.

16   Lee, Yongjei, John E. Eck, and Nicholas Corsaro. "Conclusions from the history of research into the effects of police force size on crime—1968 through 2013: a historical systematic review." Journal of Experimental Criminology 12, no. 3 (2016): 431-51. doi:10.1007/s11292-016-9269-8.

17   Jany, Libor. "More killings go unsolved in Minneapolis." Star Tribune (Minneapolis), October 16, 2016.

18   Cure Violence. "Violence Prevention Model." Accessed November 14, 2017. http://cureviolence.org/the-model/the-model/.

PLANTING THE SEEDS OF A BETTER WORLD

The ideas presented here are just the seeds of the police-free communities we have to create. Many of the alternatives we've just shared are good places to begin, and we would do well to expand their reach. We know that creating a world without police won't happen overnight. If our children and their children are to live in a world without police, we will need the courage to dream bigger, create new ways of thinking about conflict, and solve problems that we haven't even imagined yet. But we can do this. We have to. We *will*.

For 150 years, Minneapolis has been burdened by a police department that is violent, oppressive, and unaccountable. It's time for us to put an end to that chapter of our city's history and begin a new one—one without police.

MPD150'S FIVE ESSENTIAL FINDINGS

1. The police were established to protect the interests of the wealthy, and **racialized violence has always been part of that mission.**

2. The police **cannot be reformed** away from their core function.

3. The police **criminalize dark skin and poverty,** channeling millions of people into the prison system, depriving them of voting and employment rights, and thereby preserving privileged access to housing, jobs, land, credit, and education for whites.

4. The police **militarize and escalate** situations that call for social service intervention.

5. There are **viable existing and potential alternatives to policing for every area** in which police engage.

APPENDIX: RESOURCES, HANDOUTS, COMICS, AN ORAL HISTORY, AND MORE

What follows are a few of the resources that MPD150 has used at conferences, street festivals, tabling opportunities, social media, and other community outreach spaces, along with a range of additional writing and commentary not included in the original release of this report. We're including all of these materials here so that they can continue to be of use, whether by people in Minneapolis, or people elsewhere who want to take the basic ideas and adapt them to their community.

RESOURCE list

심제현

ver1 (4/3 2019)

311 information

united way -211- SOCIAL SVCS
NEED NON-EMERGENCY SVCS? TRY HERE FOR RESOURCES
THEY WON'T CALL SERVICES W/OUT CONSENT!

w/love -JHS
MH emergency **《COPE*》** 612-596-1223
* THEY MAY CHOOSE TO SEND POLICE.
SVC 612-871-5111

nat'l suicide hotline
1-800-273-TALK (8255)

TransLifeLine 877-565-8860
good for crisis & non-emergencies

TEXT: 🏳️ to: 274747 CRISIS *charges may apply

+ **POISON CONTROL** 800-222-1222
↳ STAFFED BY EXPERTS (BIO/CHEM)

MN WARMLINE
651-288-0400 txt SUPPORT to 85511
mon—sat 5:00P—10:00P
this is good for non-emergencies.

—YOU CAN ALSO— **‹learn_skills›** AND BECOME A RESOURCE!

DON'T call the police.
here are some ideas:

use these #'s!

CORRECTIONS? UPDATES? FEEDBACK?
jaehyunshim12@gmail.com

↳ SOME COSTS INCLUDE CPR TRNG!

first aid certs*

RED CROSS	$85-$123
BLUE CROSS	also FREE! (duluth)
MN SAFETY CNL	$75-$115
YMCA	$50
CPR TWIN CITIES	$54-$94

↳ * DISCLAIMER! THESE WERE FOUND THROUGH A GOOGLE SEARCH & I CANNOT VOUCH FOR THEM PERSONALLY.

[NALOXONE] NARCAN TRAINING + KITS:

RED DOOR
Steve Rummler Hope Network

612-543-5555
525 PORTLAND AV FOURTH FLOOR
M: 9-1 + F: 1-4

952-943-3937 MNTKA, MN
HOPE@RUMMLERHOPE.ORG
offers group trainings.
policy: STEVE'S LAW.

—more things to learn—
restorative justice
DE-ESCALATION

FOR YOU
☐ TO DO: READ ABOUT STEVE'S LAW

While not an official MPD150 resource, this "who to call" sheet created by a community member did inspire our own, available at MPD150.com

BUILDING A POLICE-FREE FUTURE: FREQUENTLY ASKED QUESTIONS

PRESENTED BY MPD150: *an independent, community-based initiative challenging the narrative that police exist to protect and serve. In 2017, on the 150th anniversary of the Minneapolis Police Department, the group produced a performance evaluation of the MPD based on historical research and interviews with community members. Read the full report, along with many other resources, at www.MPD150.com.*

We believe in the power, possibility, and necessity of a police-free future. We also understand, however, that this is a new idea for many people. Here are some frequently asked questions, and our responses to them.

Won't abolishing the police create chaos and crime? How will we stay safe?

Police abolition work is not about snapping our fingers and instantly defunding every department in the world. Rather, we're talking about a *process* of strategically reallocating resources, funding, and responsibility away from police and toward community-based models of safety, support, and prevention.

The people who respond to crises in our community should be the people who are best-equipped to deal with those crises. Rather than strangers armed with guns, who very likely do not live in the neighborhoods they're patrolling, we want to create space for more mental health service providers, violence prevention specialists, social workers, victim/survivor advocates, elders and spiritual leaders, neighbors and friends—all of the people who really make up the fabric of a community—to look out for one another.

But what about armed bank robbers, murderers, and supervillains?

Crime isn't random. Most of the time, it happens when someone has been unable to meet their basic needs through other means. So to really "fight crime," we don't need more cops; we need more jobs, more educational opportunities, more arts programs, more community centers, more mental health resources, and more of a say in how our own communities function.

Sure, in this transition process, we may need a small, specialized class of public servants whose job it is to respond to violence. But part of what we're talking about here is what role police play in our society. Right now, a small fraction of police work involves responding to violence; more often, they're making traffic stops, arresting petty drug users, harassing Black and Brown people, and engaging in a range of "broken windows policing" behaviors that only serve to keep more people under the thumb of the criminal justice system.

But why not fund the police *and* fund all these alternatives too? Why is it an either/or?

It's not just that police are ineffective: in many communities, they're actively harmful. The history of policing is a history of violence against the marginalized—American police departments were originally created to dominate and criminalize communities of color and poor white workers, a job they continue doing to this day. The list has grown even longer: LGBTQ folks, people with disabilities, activists—so many of us are attacked by cops on a daily basis.

(continued on page 2)

(continued from page 1)

And it's bigger than just police brutality; it's about how the prison industrial complex, the drug war, immigration law, and the web of policy, law, and culture that forms our criminal justice system has destroyed millions of lives, and torn apart families. Cops don't prevent crime; they cause it, through the ongoing, violent disruption of our communities.

It's also worth noting that most social service agencies and organizations that could serve as alternatives to the police are underfunded, scrambling for grant money to stay alive while being forced to interact with officers who often make their jobs even harder. In 2016, the Minneapolis Police Department received $165 million in city funding alone. Imagine what that kind of money could do to keep our communities safe if it was reinvested.

Even people who support the police agree: we ask cops to solve too many of our problems. As former Dallas Police Chief David Brown said: *"We're asking cops to do too much in this country... Every societal failure, we put it off on the cops to solve. Not enough mental health funding, let the cops handle it... Here in Dallas we got a loose dog problem; let's have the cops chase loose dogs. Schools fail, let's give it to the cops... That's too much to ask. Policing was never meant to solve all those problems."*

What about body cameras? What about civilian review boards, implicit bias training, and community policing initiatives?

Video footage (whether from body cameras or other sources) wasn't enough to get justice for Philando Castile, Samuel DuBose, Walter Scott, Tamir Rice, and far too many other victims of police violence. A single implicit bias training session can't overcome decades of conditioning and department culture. Other reforms, while often noble in intention, simply do not do enough to get to the root of the issue.

History is a useful guide here: community groups in the 1960s also demanded civilian review boards, better training, and community policing initiatives. Some of these demands were even met. But universally, they were either ineffective, or dismantled by the police department over time. Recent reforms are already being co-opted and destroyed: just look at how many officers are wearing body cameras that are never turned on, or how quickly Jeff Sessions' Justice Department moved to end consent decrees. We have half a century's worth of evidence that reforms can't work. It's time for something new.

This all sounds good in theory, but wouldn't it be impossible to do?

Throughout US history, everyday people have regularly accomplished "impossible" things, from the abolition of slavery, to voting rights, to the forty-hour workweek, and more. What's really impossible is the idea that the police departments can be reformed, against their will, to protect and serve communities whom they have always attacked. The police, as an institution around the world, have existed for less than 200 years—less time than chattel slavery existed in the Americas. Abolishing the police doesn't need to be difficult—we can do it in our own cities, one dollar at a time, through redirecting budgets to common-sense alternative programs. Let's get to work!

FIND MORE RESOURCES ON BUILDING A POLICE-FREE FUTURE (INCLUDING BOOK RECOMMENDATIONS, ARTICLES, TOOLKITS, AND MORE) AT WWW.MPD150.COM

10 ACTION IDEAS FOR BUILDING A POLICE-FREE FUTURE

Imagine that you were asked to help create stability in a newly founded city. How would you try to solve the problems that your friends and neighbors encountered? How would you respond to crisis and violence? Would your *first* choice be an unaccountable army with a history of oppression and violence patrolling your neighborhood around the clock? **-- from Enough Is Enough: A 150-Year Performance Review of the Minneapolis Police Department**

What makes a community healthy and safe? This document doesn't have all the answers, but it acknowledges that for many of us, police are not part of the solution. Patterns of racism, sexism, homophobia, transphobia, and bullying are too common. When someone is having a mental health crisis, or when neighbors are concerned about a fellow neighbor, or when we feel unsafe- are the police our only option? Of course, different communities have different needs. Vibrant, dynamic, and police-free communities aren't going to be created by outside groups- they're going to bloom from the soil that already exists in those spaces. What we can share here, though, is what that process has looked like elsewhere. Here are a few tools, ideas, and strategies:

1. An easy one: STOP calling the police when it's clearly unnecessary.

We can't tell you to never call the police (though some do make that choice). We can challenge you, however, to reflect on that choice, to make sure that calling them isn't an automatic response to each and every moment of personal discomfort or uncertainty. Never forget: an inconvenience for one person, once police are involved, can become a death sentence for another person.

2. Get trained in first aid, crisis de-escalation, restorative justice, etc.

The more skills we have to share with our neighbors and family, the less we have to rely on unaccountable armed paramilitary forces! Find or organize local trainings, and share that knowledge.

3. Build community all the time, not just in times of trouble.

It isn't just about building capacity as individuals; it's about cultivating resilient communities. One of the first steps we can take toward communities that no longer need police is meeting one another. We can know our neighbors' names. We can hold potlucks, volunteer to help our neighbors with simple things like shoveling snow or carrying groceries, and build real relationships. That way, when crises happen, we have other resources to call upon besides the police.

As **Critical Resistance's Abolitionist Toolkit** puts it: *It can be as simple as asking a friend a basic question: "If I needed to, could I call you?" or telling someone "If you ever needed someone, you could call me." We know that this is nothing like a perfect solution. But we have to begin to try out what solutions might work, especially because we know that calling the police doesn't.*

4. If you DO need police, go to them instead of calling them to you.

From the zine **"12 Things to Do Instead of Calling the Cops:"** *If something of yours is stolen and you need to file a report for insurance or other purposes, consider going to the police station instead of bringing cops into your community. You may inadvertently be putting someone in your neighborhood at risk.*

5. With mental health crises, remember to center the person in crisis.

From the article **"5 Ways to Help Someone in a Mental Health Emergency Without Calling the Police"** (Tastrom): *Remember that the person having the mental health crisis is a person and their wishes should be followed as much as is safe. The best intervention strategies will be things that the person buys into and does voluntarily. Those of us with mental health issues have likely been traumatized by doctors and other practitioners not listening to us or doing things against our will. All of this is contextual and there are no absolutes, but think about trauma when you are considering what actions to take.*

6. Make a list of local services/hotlines you can call instead of the police.

From domestic abuse crisis centers, to shelters for people experiencing homelessness, to mental health support groups, to a range of other kinds of advocates and service-providers, find the people who can deal with the kinds of crises that police so often are not equipped to handle. Find out which ones involve the police as a matter of protocol, and which ones don't. Hang the list on your refrigerator. Keep those contacts in your phone. Make copies and give them to friends and neighbors. **Find some examples in the MPD150 Report at www.mpd150.com!**

7. Support organizations that really do keep our communities healthy.

On that note: where these services exist, support them, whether by volunteering, donating, or lobbying for funding from city/county/etc. government. Some great alternatives to the police already exist; they're just often extremely underfunded. Take this a step further: how might we strategically re-allocate resources from police to services that truly help people? Campaigns to divest from police while investing in communities may offer a path forward.

8. Zoom in and find solutions where you are.

Across the country, activists are finding ways to change the narrative and do this work. Teachers and parents are working on campaigns like Dignity in Schools' "Counselors Not Cops." LGBTQ groups are disinviting police to Pride parades. Formerly incarcerated people are organizing networks of mentorship and even unarmed community mediation teams. Organizations like the Sex Workers Outreach Project are working to address stigma and criminalization. Churches are pledging to not call the police. From the decriminalization of drugs, to the dismantling of the school-to-prison pipeline, to abolishing ICE, and beyond- every step gets us closer to a police-free future.

9. Engage in policy work that can prevent, rather than just punish, crime.

When we ask people, "What keeps your community healthy and safe?" the answers we hear are often very similar: affordable housing, jobs, youth programs, opportunities to create and experience art, welcoming parks, etc. We can cultivate safer and healthier neighborhoods by getting involved in activist organizations, neighborhood groups, school boards, etc. that have the power to do this preventative work.

10. Dream bigger: there was a time before police, and there will be a time after.

Some of the solutions we need don't exist yet. There are some things we can do now, but this work is also about planting seeds. A vital first step toward a police-free future is simply being able to visualize what that future will look like. We must break out of the old mindset that police are this inevitable, irreplaceable part of society. They aren't. There are better ways for us to keep our communities healthy and safe, ways that do not include the violent, oppressive, unaccountable baggage of police forces. Check out the various sources mentioned here. Do more research, have more conversations, and help build the world in which you want to live.   **www.mpd150.com**

>>TRANSITION & ALTERNATIVES

MPD150 proposes:

1) Returning genuine service functions back to community control.

2) Transferring resources to address unmet needs and crises in Minneapolis.

This could look like...

>> *Don't call the police*
This won't make the problem go away, but it won't make it worse. Look to people in your community & other resources.

>> *Commit to community safety*
Take a class in de-escalation techniques, learn first aid, & organize a block party. Learn skills and build relationships.

OPEN FOR A COMIC...

>>INTERVIEWS

"I feel like the police here overdo their job... or they don't probably even do their job because I feel like the police are going and looking for reasons to arrest black people."
- Northside Resident

"I've heard officers say terrible things to victims like, 'Why do I need to be here? You're just going to go back to this person.'"
- Domestic Violence Advocate

"If you were drunk or you had a relative that was out late, most of the time if they got in trouble or beat up, it was from the police. And so we had to keep our eyes on the police."
- Native Elder

Ending 150 years of police in Minneapolis

Get Involved

info@mpd150.com
www.mpd150.com
#MPDtruth

1867-2017

MPD150

working toward a police-free Minneapolis

THIS SHOULD BE EVERYONE'S REALITY...

- Be able to walk down street
- Kids playing in the park
- [YOUR IDEA]
- Space to learn from my actions
- [YOUR IDEA]
- Guaranteed access to the things I need
- Healthy accountability for actions
- Knowing my neighbors & I will be safe

What do you want your community reality to be?

...BUT THE POLICE KEEP MANY PEOPLE FROM THIS REALITY.

2017 is the **150th anniversary** of the Minneapolis Police Dep't. In this historic moment, MPD150 is calling for a **police-free future**.

We're **researching** MPD history, **interviewing** people impacted by police, **mapping** responsible alternatives, & **creating** visionary art to make a police-free world possible.

WE KNOW WE ARE MISSING STORIES. SHARE YOURS. #MPDTRUTH

>>RESEARCH

Since **1867**, MPD has been enforcing violence against people of color & poor folks while protecting people w/ $$$.

People have tried solving issues of policing through **reforms**. But reforms are procedural & disciplinary and do not address the function or power of police.

Examples...
>>Police dep'ts are aggressively limiting public access to **body & dash camera** footage while granting it to officers under investigation.

>>Racial profiling increased in San Diego after **hiring more black cops** b/c cops of color are more closely scrutinized and often punished for speaking out.

"WE'RE ASKING COPS TO DO TOO MUCH IN THIS COUNTRY... EVERY SOCIETAL FAILURE, WE PUT IT OFF ON THE COPS TO SOLVE. NOT ENOUGH MENTAL HEALTH FUNDING, LET THE COPS HANDLE IT... HERE IN DALLAS WE GOT A LOOSE DOG PROBLEM: LET'S HAVE THE COPS CHASE LOOSE DOGS. SCHOOLS FAIL, LET'S GIVE IT TO THE COPS... THAT'S TOO MUCH TO ASK. POLICING WAS NEVER MEANT TO SOLVE ALL THOSE PROBLEMS."

--FORMER DALLAS POLICE CHIEF DAVID BROWN

It's also worth noting that most social service agencies and organizations that could serve as alternatives to the police are underfunded, scrambling for grant money to stay alive while being forced to interact with officers who often make their jobs even harder. In 2016, the Minneapolis Police Department received $165 million in city funding alone. Imagine what that kind of money could do to keep our communities safe if it was reinvested.

d it's bigger than just police brutality; it's about
w the prison industrial complex, the drug war, and
migration law, and the web of policy, law, and
ture that forms our criminal justice system has
stroyed millions of lives, and torn apart families.
ps don't prevent crime; they cause it, through
e ongoing, violent disruption of our communities.

ily basis.
tivists– so many of us are attacked by cops on a
en longer. LGBTQ folks, people with disabilities,
y continue doing to this day. The list has grown
mmunities of color and poor white workers, a job
ginally created to dominate and criminalize
rginalized– American police departments were
policing is a history of violence against the
mmunities, they're actively harmful. The history
s not just that police are ineffective: in many

HY IS IT AN EITHER/OR?
ND ALL THESE ALTERNATIVES TOO?
T WHY NOT FUND THE POLICE AND

WHAT ABOUT BODY CAMERAS? WHAT ABOUT CIVILIAN REVIEW BOARDS, IMPLICIT BIAS TRAINING, AND COMMUNITY POLICING INITIATIVES?

Video footage (whether from body cameras or other sources) wasn't enough to get justice for Philando Castile, Samuel DuBose, Walter Scott, Tamir Rice, and far too many other victims of police violence. A single implicit bias training session can't overcome decades of conditioning and department culture. Other reforms, while often noble in intention, simply do not do enough to get to the root of the issue.

History is a useful guide here: community groups in the 1960s also demanded civilian review boards, better training, and community policing initiatives. Some of these demands were even met. But universally, they were either ineffective, or dismantled by the police department over time. It's time to try something new.

THIS ALL SOUNDS GOOD IN THEORY, B WOULDN'T IT BE IMPOSSIBLE TO DO?

Throughout US history, everyday people have regularly accomplished "impossible" things, from the abolition of slavery, to voting rights, to the 40-hour workweek, and more.

What's really impossible is the idea that police departments can be reformed against their will to protect and serve communities whom they have always attacked.

The police, as an institution around the world, have existed for less than 200 years– less time than chattel slavery existed in the Americas. Abolishing the police doesn't need to be difficult– we can do it in our own cities, one dollar at a time, through redirecting budgets to common-sense alternative programs.

Let's get to work!

BUILDING A POLICE-FREE FUTURE: FREQUENTLY ASKED QUESTIONS

presented by
MPD150

MPD150 is an independent, community-based initiative challenging the narrative that police exist to protect and serve. In 2017, on the 150th anniversary of the Minneapolis Police Department, the group produced a performance evaluation of the MPD based on historical research and interviews with community members. Read the full report at www.MPD150.com.

We believe in the power, possibility, and necessity of a police-free future. We also understand, however, that this is a new idea for many people. What follows are some frequently-asked questions, and our responses.

WON'T ABOLISHING THE POLICE CREATE CHAOS AND CRIME? HOW WILL WE STAY SAFE?

Police abolition work is not about snapping our fingers and instantly defunding every department in the world. Rather, we're talking about a gradual process of strategically reallocating resources, funding, and responsibility away from police and toward community-based models of safety, support, and prevention.

The people who respond to crises in our community should be the people who are best-equipped to deal with those crises. Rather than strangers armed with guns, who very likely do not live in the neighborhoods they're patrolling, we want to create space for more mental health service providers, social workers, victim/survivor advocates, religious leaders, neighbors and friends- all of the people who really make up the fabric of a community- to look out for one another.

BUT WHAT ABOUT ARMED BANK ROBBERS, MURDERERS, AND SUPERVILLAINS?

Crime isn't random. Most of the time, it happens when someone has been unable to meet their ba[sic] needs through other means. So to really "fight crime," we don't need more cops; we need more jobs, more educational opportunities, more arts programs, more community centers, more menta[l] health resources, and more of a say in how our o[wn] communities function.

Sure, in this long transition process, we may nee[d a] small, specialized class of public servants whose [job] is to respond to violent crimes. But part of what we're talking about here is what role police play [in] our society. Right now, cops don't just respond t[o] violent crimes; they make needless traffic stops, arrest petty drug users, harass Black and Brown people, and engage in a wide range of "broken windows policing" behaviors that on[ly] serve to keep more people under th[e] thumb of the criminal justice system.

[A] FEW RESOURCES FOR FURTHER [LE]ARNING AND ACTION

[Rea]d the full MPD150 report, as well as extended [int]erview excerpts, ways to get involved, and more [at] MPD150.com.

Reading List:

The End of Policing (Alex Vitale)
The New Jim Crow (Michelle Alexander)
Are Prisons Obsolete? (Angela Y. Davis)
Abolition Now!: Ten Years of Strategy and Struggle Against the Prison Industrial Complex (Anthology)
Our Enemies in Blue: Police and Power in America (Kristian Williams)
13th & When They See Us (films by Ava DuVernay)
The study guide at aworldwithoutpolice.org
A big list of accessible, online articles and essays [i]n the "resources" tab at MPD150.com

What are we talking about when we talk about "a police-free future?"

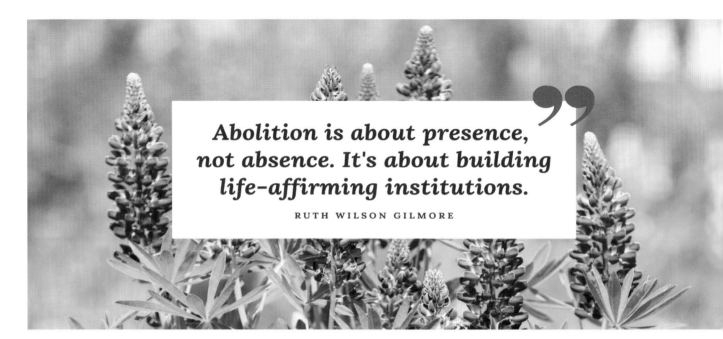

> *Abolition is about presence, not absence. It's about building life-affirming institutions.*
>
> RUTH WILSON GILMORE

Editor's note: this document was posted on the MPD150 website on June 10, 2020, as a followup to the FAQ zine on the previous pages. In the web version, each point here is accompanied by links to further reading.

This document does not speak for the whole movement, or even all organizers here in Minneapolis. Please be wary of sharing content that claims to. These are simply some thoughts, talking points, and stories that have been useful to us as we've had discussions with people in our community about abolition.

Over the past two weeks, our "Building a Police-Free Future: Frequently-Asked Questions" zine has been shared tens of thousands of times. That zine is a great first step, but it's also only 1,000 words long! We know people still have questions, especially when it comes to some of the more immediate, down-to-earth concerns about abolition.

Of course, the easy answer here is "read Angela Davis, read Mariame Kaba, read Ruth Wilson Gilmore, read all the books and articles on our resources page." Abolition is a big concept, and there is no answer we can give you right now that wraps it all up in one easy soundbite. But we still want to provide some concrete examples, and each point below is followed by yet another recommended reading (in the version posted at www.MPD150.com).

We (and so many others in this movement) don't want to just rebrand cops, or privatize cops, or make cops "nicer." The goal is a city without police, and defunding police is one tool we have to reach that goal. But what does that mean in practice? Here are ten points to keep in mind:

Invest in prevention, not punishment.

Whether you agree with abolition or not, it isn't hard to see that police are a massive draw on the wealth and resources of our communities. As council member Jeremiah Ellison said, "Our police have been bankrupting our city for years. Consistently and absolutely gutting taxpayers of money." Josie Duffy Rice, speaking on the Daily Show, put it like this: "We are funding the back end of social ills, instead of the front end of addressing them." There are smarter ways to structure our budgets.

What does "investing in prevention" look like in practice?

Some of this is big picture, like making significant, long-term changes to how our city budget addresses affordable housing, youth programs, mental health services, addiction treatment options, jobs programs, education, etc. But there are also some really concrete, specific examples of what that "prevention, not punishment" approach can look like:

- Minneapolis' Group Violence Intervention initiative has "helped de-escalate tension between groups on the north side without involving Minneapolis police."
- MN activists have called for comprehensive sex ed in schools that includes curricula on consent, bodily autonomy, and healthy relationships as a way to prevent gender-based violence.
- Minneapolis youth have organized to shift SRO (school resource officer) budgets into things like restorative justice trainings, school counselors, and more.

Many people already live in a world without police (pt. 1).

If you grew up in a well-off, predominantly white suburb, how often did you interact with cops? Communities with lots of good jobs, strong schools, economies, and social safety nets are already, in some ways, living in a world without police (of course, there's so much more to say here about gentrification, redlining, white flight, and how one function of policing is to keep these communities white, but this point is still worth considering).

Many people already live in a world without police (pt. 2).

We want to make sure everyone has someone to call on for help. It's critical to note, though, that for many of us, especially those of us living in under-resourced, Black, Indigenous, and people of color communities, the police have never been helpful. In fact, they've been a major source of harm and violence. Millions of us already live in a world where we don't even think about calling on the police for help; it isn't some kind of far-future fantasy.

Public safety is bigger than policing.

Abolitionists want everyone to be safe. We're just acknowledging that there are other ways to think about "safety" than armed paramilitary forces with a proven track record of racism, brutality, and a focus on responding to harm after it's happened rather than de-escalating or preventing it in the first place. We need to explore those "other ways," lift up current practices for building safe communities without police, and innovate some new ones too.

We're abolishing the police, not abolishing "help."

Even before 2020, there was work happening in Minneapolis to rethink how 9-1-1 works, and who gets routed where as "first responders." We want to continue that work. A world without police will still have 9-1-1. It will still have firefighters and EMTs. And across the US, there are hundreds of programs and initiatives that help people without police being the first point of contact. Check out programs like COPE in Minneapolis, CAHOOTS in Eugene, and our own list of places to call when you're in crisis (available at www.MPD150.com). Some of these programs need more support; other programs have yet to be built.

Abolition is a process, not a "Thanos snap" where all the cops just instantly disappear.

As our FAQ resource says: "Police abolition work is not about snapping our fingers and magically defunding every department in the world instantly. Rather, we're talking about a *process* of strategically reallocating resources, funding, and responsibility away from police and toward community-based models of safety, support, and prevention."

In an interview with Kare11, council member Ellison said:

"Defunding MPD, by the time we're ready to do that, we will have a fully formed new public safety strategy in place. There are things that we're going to have to do in the next couple of weeks and months, right? We've got the budget coming up. We've got this huge budget shortfall because of coronavirus. We also have other public safety strategies that are not the police that we've sort of failed to fund but they do work. Those are things that we can kind of get putting our resources behind right away. But you're right. The work of creating a whole new safety apparatus is going to take some time."

Yes, different activists will have different perspectives on this point, and we challenge people to understand why someone might indeed call for a particular police department's instant, total dissolution.

But whether a community's specific demand is to defund a department all at once, or gradually over time, the idea of abolition being a process remains the same. It will take time and effort to build the institutions and services we need, to continue to make connections between policing, prisons, immigration policy, and beyond, and to make sure we're not replicating the logic of prisons and punishment in our own solutions.

"But what about violent crimes? Who will we call?"

Prevention efforts *will* reduce the number of violent crimes. They won't stop them all, though. In our FAQ zine, we talk about how "in this long transition process, we may need a small, specialized class of public servants whose job it is to respond to violent crimes." It's important to note that that's one option, and it's an option that brings up as many questions as it answers.

Different activists, thinkers, and communities will have different responses to these questions. How can we intervene humanely and safely in high-risk situations? How do we ensure that those people trained and entrusted to do this work during the transition process do not become "police" with a different name? How might different communities be empowered to decide for themselves what they need, whether that's AIM patrols, community mutual aid efforts, transformative justice programs, and/or governmental solutions?

A bigger takeaway here is that however you respond to the "what about violent crimes?" question, it doesn't make sense to structure our entire, multi-billion dollar social safety apparatus around that relatively rare class of behaviors. As a country, we don't need to spend $80 billion on prisons to deal with the small handful of serial killers for whom restorative justice isn't going to work. We don't need to spend $100 billion on police because of the fact that prevention efforts (many of which we haven't even tried yet) aren't able to stop 100% of all harm that human beings inflict on each other.

This new world won't be perfect. But we have to see how imperfect the current world is.

Will a focus on prevention magically stop all harm? Of course not. But we have to ask: how much harm is our current system stopping? How many murders, or sexual assaults, do police currently "solve," much less prevent? Here in Minnesota, we had a whole multi-part series in our local paper on "how Minnesota's criminal justice system has failed victims of sexual assault," and lots of people have already seen the statistics on how, when it comes to sexual violence, "the vast majority of perpetrators will not go to jail or prison." Redirecting resources into prevention efforts won't solve all of our problems, but it's a common sense step we can and should take that will have a real impact on people's lives.

"Abolition is about presence, not absence. It's about building life-affirming institutions." -Ruth Wilson Gilmore

That's a quote we return to often, especially when we're feeling uncertain.

It's true: there is some uncertainty ahead of us. As we've been saying, some of what we need to live in a police-free future, we already have; some, we have to build. As Minneapolis considers its future, know that the question isn't just "cops or no cops." The question is a much deeper, more fundamental one about what we build in their place. That's going to involve a lot of community meetings, budget hearings, and neighbors talking to neighbors. It's going to be hard. It's going to take constant community buy-in and pressure on elected leaders.

But all of the uncertainty ahead of us is still a better choice than the status quo. The status quo is a Black man calling out for his mother as a police officer kneels on his neck. The status quo is a seemingly never-ending list of names, hashtags, and lives cut short—not just by police violence, but by the ongoing violence of a system that cages millions of people and tears apart families. The status quo is the ongoing harassment and intimidation of communities going about their daily lives and simply existing.

That's the work ahead of us. A police-free future isn't something that just happens to us; it's something we build, together.

Further reading: check out the big Resources page at www.MPD150.com, including book recommendations, more articles, and a whole section featuring just writing from the 2020 Uprising. There's also the "alternatives" section of our report, featuring a few more specific programs and ideas. And as always, be sure to check out Reclaim the Block and Black Visions Collective to get plugged into this work in Minneapolis, as it happens.

A selection of artwork and panels from MPD150's "Making It Real" art exhibit (October 2018)

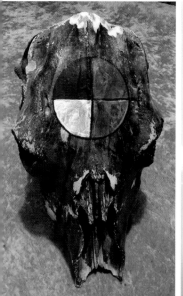

Pieces by Aja Marie Ussrey (clockwise from top left): "Bovine," "The Trickster," "Red Dress," and "The Red Road."

The "Making It Real" exhibit was arranged like this report, around the past, present, and future. Of these pieces, "The Red Road" represented the past, "Red Dress" the present, and "Trickster" the future.

An artist who chose not to be named created this photo collage of the abundance of non-police resources that Minneapolis has to call upon.

Photo sections include "Community Builders," "Cultural Change Makers," "Educators," and more.

The Futile Cycle of Police Reform

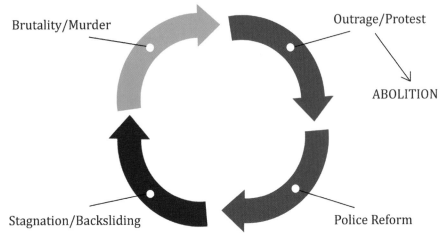

Brutality/Murder

Outrage/Protest

ABOLITION

Stagnation/Backsliding

Police Reform

The upper two images are taken from Ja[...] Yeates and Sishir Bommakanti's, "A D[...] Blue History." On the left, a physical [...] that exhibit visitors could pick up and l[...] through, along with framed prints; on [...] right, an image from the zine.

Another artist, Ali, contributed an inte[...] tive installment that we cannot repli[...] here. We'd like to thank all of the artists [...] helped make the "Making It Real" exh[...] well, real.

On the (direct) left: "The Futile Cycle of [...] lice Reform" (panel via MPD150)

On the right: "The Minneapolis Police Oversight Graveyard" (panel via MPD150)

For more context for this image, check out the timeline pieces on pages 74-76 of this report.

THE MINNEAPOLIS POLICE OVERSIGHT GRAVEYARD

Civilian Review Board 1963 – 1963

Civil Rights Commission 1967 – 1971

Civilian Review Authority 1991 – 2012

Police Community Relations Council 2003 – 2008

Office of Police Conduct Review 2012 – ?

Minneapolis Police chased Thurman Blevins 'several blocks' before fatal shooting

Monday, June 25, 2018 by Mike Mullen in News

Minneapolis Police were called to a location several blocks from where they found Thurman Blevins; they chased him several blocks more before shooting him.

*Officer Jeronimo Yanez, photographed just after shooting and killing Philando Castile.
Courtesy of the Minnesota Bureau of Criminal Apprehension*

The New York Times

Ketamine Used to Subdue Dozens at Request of Minneapolis Police, Report Says

Minneapolis police officers asked emergency medical responders to use the tranquilizer ketamine to sedate suspects and others who were restrained, The Star Tribune reported.   Mark Zdechlik/MPR News

By Christopher Mele

June 16, 2018

Minneapolis cop receives 4 years for sexual assault

Tim Nelson · Minneapolis · May 30, 2018   Issues

A former Minneapolis police officer has been sentenced to four years in prison for sexually assaulting an unconscious woman in northeast Minneapolis two years ago.

Thomas Tichich, 49, was convicted of third degree criminal sexual conduct and attempted sexual assault by a Hennepin County jury in April.

The victim, a 39-year-old woman at the time of the assault the night of Dec. 14, 2016, told the court that she had suffered from "fear, pain, anxiety and emotional distress," during the ordeal, and that "testifying in court reopened my wounds all over again." She did not speak to his sentence however.

Thomas Robert Tichich Hennepin County Sheriff's Office

*The Way,
1913 Plymouth Avenue
Courtesy of the Minnesota
Historical Society*

The first board members of the American Indian Movement (AIM), 1968.

Photograph by Roger Woo, courtesy of the American Indian Movement Interpretative Center.

A woman at a podium speaks into a microphone as audience members look on, 1968.

Photograph by Roger Woo, courtesy of the American Indian Movement Interpretative Center.

In the wake of the 1967 riot, the Black community created the Black Patrol and the Soul Force, community safety agencies inspired by the Black Panther Party. The Native community followed suit in 1968, coming together on Plymouth Avenue and founding the American Indian Movement and its community safety agency, the AIM Patrol. All of these groups were ran by members from the communities they served, and they played a major role in making folks safer, especially from police brutality.

53

MPD150 EDUCATOR TOOLKIT

Planting the Seeds of a Police-Free Future

This document contains a few readings, resources, and potential activities for teachers and other educators interested in introducing abolition to their students.

WHO IS THIS FOR?

The materials presented here are tools. If an educator is working with middle school students, vs. college undergrads, vs. some other group, that educator can make the call with regards to which materials to use, and how those materials might fit with their students and/or their pedagogical style.

We'd like this toolkit to be useful to educators from a variety of disciplines and backgrounds, but it will likely be especially relevant for:

• *Social Studies and History classes,* especially in the Twin Cities area, since the MPD150 report is largely about Minneapolis.

• *Language Arts, Speech, and English classes,* as the report is a useful example of persuasive writing, with a clear thesis statement, supporting materials, and call to action.

• *Any class with a Critical Thinking emphasis.* The MPD150 report is about a specific issue, but it's also about the larger idea of expanding our imaginations, challenging what is framed as "radical" or "common sense," and encouraging us all to interrogate dominant narratives about crime, punishment, and safety.

• *Study groups, popular education spaces, informal dialogues, and beyond.* Education doesn't just happen in the classroom. We hope these materials, and this entire report, will be useful to everyone as we continue to have conversations and expand our thinking around these issues.

Art by Jared Ingebretson and Nikki Ann

RESOURCES AVAILABLE AT WWW.MPD150.COM

MPD150's "ENOUGH IS ENOUGH" REPORT is available as a PDF for online viewing, an audio version featuring multiple voices reading the report aloud (also available via podcast apps), and a physical document.

MPD150's "FREQUENTLY ASKED QUESTIONS" ZINE is potentially useful as "intro" material, since it's shorter and more easily digestible than the full report. Two versions are included in this report (p. 40-41 & p. 46-47)

"COMMUNITY POLICING AND OTHER FAIRY TALES" COMIC BOOK is a comic book collaboration between MPD150 and a crew of incredibly talented artists and writers. It's included in this report (starting on page 86), and is also available as a standalone text.

DOWNLOADABLE POSTERS: Feel free to print them out for use in interactive gallery spaces, or as visual aids for presentations and discussions. A few examples are included in this report (p. 52-53)

ADDITIONAL READINGS AND RESOURCES: We've tried to pull together a range of books, accessible online articles (including many local examples), and other toolkits on the Resources page at our website. This can be a good starting point for students doing research projects. A few highlights:

The African American Intellectual History Society's Prison Abolition Syllabus contains a wealth of readings and a potential curriculum arc: *www.aaihs.org/prisonabolition-syllabus-2-0.*

Critical Resistance is a pioneer in this work, and their Abolitionist Toolkit contains readings, discussion questions, and more: *www.criticalresistance.org/wpcontent/uploads/2012/06/CR-Abolitionist-Toolkit-online.pdf*

MPD150 is an independent, community-based initiative challenging the narrative that police exist to protect and serve. In 2017, on the 150th anniversary of the Minneapolis Police Department, the group produced a performance evaluation of the MPD based on historical research and interviews with community members. Read the full report at www.mpd150.com.

We believe in the power, possibility, and necessity of a police-free future. This toolkit is for educators who understand the importance of critical thinking and imagination, especially in the context of the school-to-prison pipeline, mass incarceration, and police violence. This is for educators who understand that we need to tell a better story about justice, safety, and community, and that the next generation has a vital, central role in telling that story. We hope you will find something useful here.

AMPLE DISCUSSION QUESTIONS (ON AUTHORITY):

ulled from a bank of questions by Standing Up for Racial Justice - SURJ)

What were you taught about rules? How did you know the rules, what was pected of you, what was appropriate or inappropriate?

What happened when you broke the rules or acted out of what was expected you? Were you punished? Did you see others being punished?

What happened when people who were different from you acted out or broke e rules? ("different"can refer to race, gender or any other kind of difference).

What happens now when you imagine getting in trouble or disappointing meone?

What were your relationships like with adults growing up? With teachers? 'hat were you taught about teachers?

What were you taught respect looks like?

Who had power in your community? In your family? How were you taught behave in relationship to them?

Who were you taught to see as an authority? How were you taught to behave relationship to them?

How did adults/people in power respond to you when you questioned uthority?

SAMPLE DISCUSSION QUESTIONS (ON POLICING):

• When you hear the word "police," what do you notice in your body?

• What is your first memory of police?

• What were you taught about police?

• How were you taught to behave in relationship to them?

• What did you witness or experience that impacted how you feel about the police?

• Do you feel safe when police arrive on a scene? Have you ever?

• What is a lie/false narrative you were given about police?

• What truth that you hold dear does the current system/police/etc. violate/challenge?

• (For groups with some experience with police): What letter grade would you give your local police department? Why?

• What sustains life in our community? What keeps us healthy and safe?

• What will it be like to live in a world without police?

  ○ What do you see when you're walking down the street? Sights, smells, sounds?

  ○ How would you live or act differently?

  ○ What would be different about the city?

  ○ What are some examples of how people might treat each other?

  ○ Where would the police budget go?

• What is the stated purpose of the "Enough Is Enough" report?

• How did its writers go about fulfilling that purpose?

• If you had to summarize the report, what is the main argument that it makes about police and policing?

• Identify one moment from the "Past" section that stuck out or stayed with you. What was it? Why was it significant or interesting to you?

• Identify one quote or testimonial from the "Present" section that stuck out or stayed with you. What was it? Why was it significant or interesting to you?

• Identify one idea or proposal from the "Future" section that stuck out or stayed with you. What was it? Why was it significant or interesting to you?

• Identify the "dominant narrative" in the US regarding policing. How does the report push back against that narrative?

• What evidence does it present; what arguments does it make?

• Can you imagine a world without police? What questions do you still have about it?

• Police abolition is not a "snap your fingers and all the cops disappear" proposition. What will it take to get our communities ready for a world without police? What can we start building today?

How might you personally be able to contribute to that work? What would "plugging in" look like for you?

SAMPLE ACTIVITY: WHAT KEEPS OUR COMMUNITIES SAFE AND HEALTHY?

This is a zine-oriented writing prompt.

1. Do an online search for the "foldy zine" format, which uses one sheet of paper to make an eight-page booklet. These zines are copyable, tradeable, and inexpensive.

2. Give your zine a cover/title; it can be the title of the prompt, or something else. It could be "What Keeps My Community Safe?" or "What I Would Do with the Police Budget." It could also be something as simple as "Where I'm From," mirroring the writing prompt that many poets and teaching artists use.

3. On each page of your zine, write or draw one thing that makes your community—your neighborhood, your block, even your household—safe and healthy. For example:

  ○ Natural: parks, trees, animals, other green features.
  ○ Cultural: music, art, food, etc.
  ○ Personal: specific friends or people you value.
  ○ Organizational: resources, groups, or places that do good work.
  ○ Intangible: feelings, ideas, memories, etc.

• After students create (and potentially share/trade their zines with one another), a potential discussion could emerge: do police make us safer? Did anyone include police in their zines? What will it take to invest in all the things that do make our communities healthy and safe? Are we making those investments now?

SAMPLE ACTIVITY: ENVISIONING A POLICE-FREE WORLD

This is an activity aimed at taking the sometimes abstract idea of abolition and making it real.

Before the workshop, draw a grid on the board with four columns and five rows.

  ° In one column, write five problems/issues/ situations (for example: mental health crisis, domestic abuse, theft, gun crimes, and traffic/ speeding/car violations)

  ° In the next column: "how police handle these situations"

  ° In the next column: "other ways people could potentially handle these situations"

  ° In the last column: "how do we prevent these situations in the first place?"

It is good to prep example responses to every box in the grid, just in case a particular group is more quiet.

Start by doing one row together. For example, for traffic/speeding violations, walk through each column: how do police handle speeding violations? What other ways could we, as a society, handle them? How could we prevent those violations in the first place?

For the other four issues/problems, break up into four small groups, having each each group focus on one. Use post-it notes to allow the groups to slowly fill in the grid.

Process/discuss, group-by-group.

When we examine how police respond to problems, what common themes do you notice?

Were you surprised by any of the ideas that people came up with for dealing with problems?

Were there any exciting or interesting breakthroughs?

A police-free world doesn't necessarily mean a perfect world. What new problems might arise? How might we tackle those?

SAMPLE ACTIVITY: "ENOUGH IS ENOUGH" DISCUSSION

Aside from the discussion questions included earlier, this is just a potential way to structure a conversation (whether as a class, in small groups, or as individual writing prompts) about what students have read.

Summarize: a collaborative summary of the report. What is the report? Who created it? Why does it exist? What did it say?

Validate: What is your immediate reaction to the report? Without analyzing or judging it, what single word or phrase comes to mind after you've read it?

Question: What questions do you still have based on your reading? A big collaborative list of questions can be fertile ground for continuing conversation, or continuing research!

Analyze: Identify a particular argument, moment, or passage from the report that resonates strongly with you. Why does it?

Create: Based on your reactions, your questions, and your analysis, what could you potentially create to "add on" to the report? Would it be more interviews? A deeper dive into the history? A similar project but with a different city? Or maybe a policy/lobby/organizing idea based on the report's findings?

Brainstorm what might come next.

Depending on the class, that "brainstorm" might become a project.

POETRY AND POSSIBILITY

The following pages contain five poems written by Twin Cities-based poets. Art—and poetry especially—can be such a useful entry point for exploring ideas and thinking critically, often because our responses to art don't begin or end with just intellectual engagement. Our responses can be emotional. They can be about memory and experience. They can also be active—a poem might spark some reflection and dialogue, or it might spark another poem, or some other artistic response.

MPD150 is endlessly thankful to the poets who contributed work here—these poems are powerful, as are the poems that have yet to be written.

Could we please give the police departments to the grandmothers?

BY JUNAUDA PETRUS

Could we please give the police departments to the grandmothers? Give them the salaries and the pensions and the city vehicles, but make them a fleet of vintage corvettes, jaguars and cadillacs, with white leather interior. Diamond in the back, sunroof top and digging the scene with the gangsta lean.

Let the cars be badass!

You would hear the old-school jams like Patti Labelle, Anita Baker, and Al Green. You would hear Sweet Honey in the Rock harmonizing on "We who believe in freedom will not rest" bumping out the speakers.

And they got the booming system.

If you up to mischief, they will pick you up swiftly in their sweet ride and look at you until you catch shame and look down at your lap. She asks you if you are hungry and you say "yes" and of course you are. She got a crown of dreadlocks and on the dashboard you see brown faces like yours, shea buttered and loved up.

And there are no precincts.

Just love temples, that got spaces to meditate and eat delicious food. Mangoes, blueberries, nectarines, cornbread, peas and rice, fried plantain, fufu, yams, greens, okra, pecan pie, salad and lemonade.

Things that make your mouth water and soul arrive.

All the hungry bellies know warmth, all the children expect love. The grandmas help you with homework, practice yoga with you and teach you how to make jamabalaya and coconut cake. From scratch.

When you're sleepy she will start humming and rub your back while you drift off. A song that she used to have the record of when she was your age. She remembers how it felt like to be you and be young and not know the world that good. Grandma is a sacred child herself, who just circled the sun enough times into the ripeness of her cronehood.

She wants your life to be sweeter.

When you are wildin' out because your heart is broke or you don't have what you need, the grandmas take your hand and lead you to their gardens. You can lay down amongst the flowers. Her grasses, roses, dahlias, irises, lilies, collards, kale, eggplants, blackberries. She wants you know that you are safe and protected, universal limitless, sacred, sensual, divine and free.

Grandma is the original warrior, wild since birth, comfortable in loving fiercely. She has fought so that you don't have to, not in the same ways at least.

So give the police departments to the grandmas—they are fearless, classy and actualized. Blossomed from love. They wear what they want and say what they please.

Believe that.

There wouldn't be noise citations when the grandmas ride through our streets, blasting Stevie Wonder, Nina Simone, Marvin Gaye, Alice Coltrane, Jimi Hendrix, KRS-One. All that good music. The kids gonna hula hoop to it and sell her lemonade made from heirloom pink lemons and maple syrup. The car is solar powered and carbon footprint-less; the grandmas designed the technology themselves.

At night they park the cars in a circle so all can sit in them with the sun roofs down, and look at the stars, talk about astrological signs, what to plant tomorrow based on the moon's mood and help you memorize Audre Lorde and James Baldwin quotes. She always looks you in the eye and acknowledges the light in you with no hesitation or fear. And Grandma loves you fiercely forever.

She sees the pain in our bravado, the confusion in our anger, the depth behind our coldness. Grandma know what oppression has done to our souls and is gonna change it one love temple at a time. She has no fear.

for philando

BY TONY THE SCRIBE

I walked by the governor's mansion yesterday,
memories of love and community and danger pressing on my heart.

somehow, I was still expecting to see crowds, to see tents, to see fists.

instead, a few cardboard signs fluttered in the wind like empty hands,
and a bouquet of flowers marked *philando* bent to the will of a warm breeze,
cut from their roots and displayed lovingly.

I still have trouble with how beautiful a cemetery can be.

if you go to the place where jamar clark breathed his last,
you can see balloons. cards. they say if you listen long enough,
you can hear the trees whispering "you will not be forgotten."

I wonder if this is all there is, if we will keep consecrating these spaces until none remain, if decades from now all of the trees
and grass in this city will be covered in signs and flowers and balloons. if every space will feel heavy and sodden and charged.

perhaps they already are, have been for centuries.

maybe it's just that we don't listen.

I don't understand how grief can be this beautiful. How I can wear a crown of clouds on such a sunny day. How I can die
over and over again in the midst of so much life. How I can live, day after day, in the midst of so much death.

I murmur to myself, something more than an apology but less than a prayer.

I keep it moving.

Lucky

BY ALEXEI MOON CASSELLE

*Dedicated to Philando, and everyone
who fails to see him in their mirror.*

Minneapolis is covered with tattoos
our skin is running
out of room
for names of the dead.

Maybe my name
will be immortalized in someone's
mortal flesh
for my own untimely ending
after a traffic stop gone wrong

Or
maybe I'm just

Lucky

dad didn't dye
my DNA
dark as his.

Lucky

mom's people
painted my pigment
a pale shade.

Lucky

I don't fit the description of a victim
or a fist of resistance
fighting 'gainst a primitive system

Lucky

my skin tone don't trigger
no hair-trigger response
from Them,
somehow more frightened
than the people
Them aiming at,
ready to paint the street
with their deepest,
darkest
secrets.

Lucky

the odds my daughter
will witness death
from the backseat
for broken tail light,
or being brown on Friday night,
could be worse.

Lucky

I can code switch
and shape shift
like a phantom.

Lucky

That Good Hair
keep me out the crosshairs, don't it?

Lemme ask you this:
You light skinned, mixed
mullatto, red boned, high yellow
fella:
Where'd you get that blood from, huh?

Jackson got a twenty.
Jesus got a cross.
Philando got a hashtag.

Should we
start holding funerals
for the next
viral video?

Have students write poems
on the bullets
that will plant red roses
in brown bodies?
Gather family
to paint murdered murals
on brick walls
of our unborn suspects?

Are we not convinced
the machine
we built this country with
still needs to be fed?
Jaws still gaping,
salivating,
hungry?

As black backs
for whiplash,
hungry?

for flesh,
hungry?

The monster we created,
the myth we made,
the bones in our closet,
strange fruit
hungry.

Old habits
die hard
black bodies
die young.

I can read your fortune
if you show me
your palms.
Or
you can turn your palms
face down,
so I can see
your pigment,
and I'll tell you
what your chances are.

Police make the best poets

BY KYLE "GUANTE" TRAN MYHRE

Note the creative phrasing, the novel juxtaposition of words: *the officer discharged his weapon, striking the individual*. Note how the poem is so well-constructed, the newspapers print it as-is.

Note how they call it *a perfect storm of human error;* poetry is weather, after all, not climate. Note this attention to detail: height, weight, what size pants he wore, the specific model of toy gun. Poetry is, after all, about zooming in on these concrete particulars. Note how precise they are with their cuts: history, context, connections, trends—they focus only on what is *necessary*—so every time we hear the poem, it feels fresh again.

Note their mastery of repetition. Note how they show all the things they cannot tell.

For Ahmaud et al.

BY TISH JONES

tears collapse on top of your skin like heavy rain. there is wailing all around you,
when you are born, it is a good thing. we celebrate
the hurried and uncertain attempts to breathe. we cradle you and caress your brown skin.
momentarily, we forget the trauma inherent in your blood

when you are born—it is a good thing. we celebrate
the ancestors' prayer manifest, in the flesh,
momentarily. we forget about the trauma inherent in your blood—
our blood—we imagine you living past twenty-three:

the ancestors' prayer, manifest, in the flesh.
a future where someone with skin like yours, like soot, like soil, never meets the barrel of a white man's gun.
our blood, we imagine you living past twenty-three.
anomaly:

a future where someone with skin like yours, like soot, like soil, never meets the barrel of a white man's gun.
our dreams constantly clipped at the wings. we Black—no
anomaly,
lucky to be alive. we live as who it coulda been.

our dreams constantly clipped at the wings—we Black. know
any moment is one in which a white man might want to claim scared, and shoot,
we lucky to be alive. we live as who it coulda been,
stomaching survivor's guilt like a bad secret. only, we know

any moment is one in which a white man might want to claim scared and shoot.
you did not deserve this,
stomaching survivor's guilt like a bad secret only we know.
so much of us dies with each of you.

you did not deserve this.
the hurried and uncertain attempts to breathe. we cradle you and caress your brown skin.
much of us dies with each of you.
tears collapse on top of your skin like heavy rain- there is wailing all around you.

Editorial counterpoint: We must look beyond police for community safety

Originally appeared in the Star Tribune: 3/21/19

By Tony Williams, Leilah Abdennabi, and Sheila Nezhad

As community leaders calling for less funding for police and more funding for alternative community safety measures, we were glad to see the Star Tribune Editorial Board reflecting on the relationship between police and public safety a few weeks ago ("Defunding cops is not the answer," March 8). Unfortunately, we disagree with many of the points raised.

In the spirit of robust public debate, we'd like to share more about why we have become convinced that to ensure the long-term safety of our communities, we must look beyond police.

The Minneapolis Police Department receives $189 million in funding from the city each year, supplementing that funding with other revenue sources. That's more than our Health Department, Department of Civil Rights, and Community Planning and Economic Development combined ($159.8 million). How are those resources being spent?

In 2018 alone, the Minneapolis Police Department came under fire for killing Thurman Blevins and Travis Jordan. They pressured EMS personnel to drug community members with ketamine. They set up a series of stings to entrap poor black men for low-level marijuana sales, in a state that nears closer to legalization each day. And they utterly failed, as evidenced by a powerful series in the Star Tribune, to properly investigate dozens, if not hundreds, of sexual assault cases.

Minneapolis isn't alone—racism, corruption and brutality are common in police departments across the country.

So why do we keep treating the police as if they are the one true path to community safety? It isn't true, as the Editorial Board suggests, that police are the most cost-effective way to keep our communities safe. Decades of social science research have revealed that the biggest contributor to violent crime is poverty, while a 2016 meta analysis of hundreds of studies by Yongjei Lee, John Eck and Nicholas Corsaro found that the relationship between police force size and crime levels isn't statistically significant.

As public health experts have been saying for centuries, an ounce of prevention is worth a pound of cure. A police-first approach to public safety fails to address the underlying causes of crime, while contributing to our status as the most incarcerated country in the world, and one with incredibly high levels of police violence. Why don't we try something different?

We applaud the recent decision by the Minneapolis City Council to prioritize creating an Office of Violence Prevention over hiring more staff into a scandal-ridden police department. We are confident that innovative public health approaches will prove more productive and cost-effective than policing in Minneapolis. They certainly have in other cities around the country, which have embraced programs like the "Cure Violence" model, seeing huge decreases in shootings (41 percent to 73 percent, according to studies by the Centers for Disease Control and Prevention, Northwestern and Johns Hopkins) with targeted investments.

We, and our fellow activists around the country, aren't seeking "payback" for aggressive policing. We're seeking a more effective, fiscally responsible way to keep our communities safe; one that intersects with our righteous outrage at police violence and mass incarceration.

And we have to—history shows us that police departments are incredibly resistant to reform. "Enough Is Enough: 150 Years of the Minneapolis Police

Department," a community report released in 2017, clearly demonstrates that community members have been protesting police violence here in Minneapolis for more than a century, and the proposed solutions have been universally ineffective (as with body cameras) or purposefully dismantled by police union lobbying efforts (as with the Civilian Review Agency).

In a city where police more often feel like a threat than a trusted ally, we deserve better ways to stay safe. That is why we, and our counterparts in cities around the country, are calling for a realignment of our priorities. We've increased police budgets every year in recent memory. It's long past time we stopped subsidizing the ineffectiveness and violence of policing in America and started investing in public safety solutions led by the real experts: those who are most impacted.

"Fund Communities, Not Cops" is more than a powerful slogan—it's smart policy, and we should take it as a moral mandate.

Tony Williams, Leilah Abdennabi and Sheila Nezhad are equity advocates in Minneapolis.

"Fund Communities, Not Cops" is more than a powerful slogan—it's smart policy, and we should take it as a moral mandate.

On Community Policing: Whose Community?

MPD150

What it is

When police are in the news for something bad, whether that's brutality, profiling, or other kinds of misconduct, we often hear calls for more "community policing." The image of the cop walking his beat, knowing the names of the people in the neighborhood, and becoming a trusted member of the community—this is an attractive story for a lot of people. But it's also full of holes.

"Community policing" is a police strategy meant to counter community suspicion and hostility caused by police racism, violence, and harassment. It arose alongside the increased impoverishment of Black, brown and poor communities as the "friendly face" of racialized mass incarceration. It is a strategy to calm the outrage of communities facing structural injustice while suppressing efforts to challenge that injustice. It's about optics, not meaningful policy.

Community policing is designed to create positive relationships between the police and people in the community. These "positive relationships," however, don't change the material conditions of the community, or affect the deeply rooted racism at the core of so many police departments. What they really do is provide the police with detailed information about the community, develop a cadre of community leaders who can be tapped when police actions spark public anger, and create a political support base for the police. This relationship-building is paired with an increasing reliance on military-style SWAT teams, surprise raids, and anonymous tips.

How it started

Community policing was born in response to the urban uprisings and protest movements sweeping the country in the mid-1960s. Violent police and FBI repression successfully destroyed the most militant organizations of the time, but at great cost to their legitimacy in the eyes of large segments of the population. Police looked to military "counterinsurgency" and "pacification" methods for answers.

They began to add helicopters, body armor, sophisticated weaponry, and advanced surveillance ability to the police arsenal. This steadily expanded in the 1970s and was widely embraced by the police establishment in the 1980s, a time when the threat was not from organized rebellion but from deep resentment of an economic environment of massive upward distribution of wealth from poor, Black and brown communities to the rich (called "restructuring" in the language of politicians). Instead of just targeting oppositional organizations, the police focus shifted to controlling entire communities. They also identified the need to "re-brand" as a trusted community partner.

"The predominant ways of utilizing police and law enforcement within a COIN [counterinsurgency] strategy... consist of the adoption of the community-policing approach supported by offensive policing actions such as paramilitary operations, counter-guerrilla patrolling... and raids." –excerpt from "Policing and Law Enforcement in COIN: The Thick Blue Line" (Joint Special Operations University Report, 2009)

"Patrol officers form a bond of trust with local residents who get to know them as more than a uniform. The police work with local groups, businesses, churches, and the like to address the concerns and problems of the neighborhood. Pacification is simply an expansion of this concept to include greater development and security assistance." –excerpt from the RAND corporation's "War By Other Means" report on counterinsurgency study, 2006.

How it works

Community policing is about developing personal relationships with cops—via police/youth sports and social activities, cops on bikes, visible acts of charity, precinct open houses and "officer friendly" visits to classrooms. Additionally, the police cultivate neighborhood watch and block club networks, and build relationships with neighborhood (usually homeowner) organizations, attending their meetings, listening to their concerns, and providing safety trainings that rely on police involvement.

The image they seek to promote is one of police as community friends, promoting safety and connection, reducing crime and practicing "soft" problem-solving. Because of the gentler, kinder image, communities subject to police violence often demand community policing in the hope of getting some relief from police violence.

The result (and the main goal) is a steady inflow of information to the police. Counterinsurgency/community policing relies on centralized databases and mapping out the "human terrain" of the community. The "information sharing" between police and community flows in only one direction. Human sources are supplemented with sophisticated surveillance technology, public security cameras, and social media stalking.

The "problem-solving" aspect of community policing leads to a concentration of social service functions added to police duties, functions that would be better served by community-rooted organizations that do not have the repressive social control mission of the police. The police's mission has, from the beginning, involved defending privileged white access to resources and opportunities, and the protection of the holders of wealth against the demands of the poor.

The soft methods of community policing are introduced alongside paramilitary SWAT teams. These rapid response police squads are separate from the friendly neighborhood cops so when they break down doors and terrorize people (often based on anonymous tips), the officer friendlies are on hand to reassure their community contacts and smooth things over.

Community policing does not replace racial profiling and street harassment; it enables them by recruiting community leaders to defend the police based on personal relationships with individual cops. These personal interactions promote the message "see, all cops aren't bad" and divert attention from a systemic understanding of the police role.

Broken windows policing—in which people are pursued for very minor infractions on the theory that it will prevent bigger crimes—can overlap with community policing by sending the message that it pays to stay on the good side of the cops through cooperation so as not to get the "suspect" treatment. This police tactic is often employed to make life uncomfortable for "undesirables" when a neighborhood is being gentrified.

"The research shows that community policing does not empower communities in meaningful ways. It expands police power, but does nothing to reduce the burden of overpolicing on people of color and the poor. It is time to invest in communities instead." –excerpt from "The End of Policing" by Alex S. Vitale.

Why Minneapolis doesn't need more police

by Ricardo Levins Morales (originally appeared in City Pages, 12/4/19)

When I came into the kitchen that dark Chicago morning, my father broke the news to me straight away. "They murdered Fred Hampton."

The police had stormed his apartment at 4 a.m., guns blazing. They concentrated their fire on the bedroom where they knew Hampton, the young, charismatic chairman of the city's Black Panther chapter, would be laid out flat, immobilized by the sedative an informant had slipped into his juice. Papi had just come back from the scene.

This December 4, on the 50th anniversary of Fred Hampton's assassination, the Minneapolis City Council is holding a public budget hearing featuring a plan to hire 14 more police officers at a cost of $8.5 million. Five decades ago, police departments operated under the authority of city governments, most notably serving as enforcers for corrupt political machines. That was then. With the decline of the machines in the '70s, the police emerged as the most powerful section of municipal governments, more influenced by Homeland Security, regional fusion centers, and a police equipment industry aggressively pushing the latest in weapons and surveillance systems.

While politicians turn over every few years, the police have built an enduring base of support, unwavering in its belief that more cops mean more safety. As a result, their numbers, budgets, and clout have steadily increased over the years, as racial and economic inequality have grown.

Elected backers of police expansion like Minneapolis City Council members Linea Palmisano, Lisa Goodman, and Alondra Cano seem to believe they would be supporting a community-oriented police department spearheaded by Chief Medaria Arrodondo. That department is a mirage. They would be better off investing in a unicorn park. Reformist chiefs have at best a fleeting impact on their departments, their effort—what former Minneapolis Police chief Tony Bouza called his "futile attempt to reform the police"—erased within a year or two of their departure.

Police departments in this country were consolidated as a system, in the aftermath of Emancipation, to address the urgent "problem" of how to keep black people in servitude.

The solution was a system of unequal laws, unequal enforcement, and unequal consequences to permanently stamp blacks and other unworthies with criminal records that effectively remove them from competition for good jobs, housing, credit, and education as well as barring them from voting, running for office, or serving on juries.

The true face of the Minneapolis Police Department is not Chief Arradondo, its appointed administrator, perched lightly on the iceberg of entrenched power. It is its elected leader, currently police union honcho Bob Kroll. The recent "Cops for Trump" stunt was a public endorsement by the MPD's rank and file of Donald Trump's ideology of racial, misogynist, and religious bigotry. While it can be said that not all cops share these sentiments, there's little room for dissent in police culture.

On the evening of November 12, my council member, Alondra Cano, hosted a community safety meeting for a section of her ninth ward. Earlier that day, Minneapolis cops (who insist they are too underfunded to answer 911 calls or process rape kits) raided homeless encampments in the ward in 12 degree weather, throwing away people's belongings and directing them to shelter beds that were not prepared or sufficient. KSTP's glowing account—"Minneapolis Police Department helping the homeless stay warm"—must have come straight from MPD's public relations team.

Our city representatives can choose to live in the comforting world of press releases, but the poor and displaced of our city do not have that option. They experience the real MPD in all its Trumpian power and arrogance. To view the police as a solution for social problems is to accept the premise that their brutal and racist record is the result of individual implicit bias or insufficient training in an otherwise noble institution. In other words, it requires a reckless disregard for history.

The police narrative of being the "thin blue line" against crime and chaos gives them powerful leverage over elected representatives. It is easy for them to trigger public fear, so it is never politically safe to stand up to their demands. All it would take is one shooting in your ward and you get blamed for not supporting "the brave men and women who put their lives on the line every day to keep us safe."

I can hear some saying, "But we must support our first black police chief!" Actually, we must support concrete community safety practices that have a real chance for success. Implicit bias training, civilian review commissions (we're on our fifth!), cops on bikes or handing out ice cream cones, even putting more dark people and women in charge—none of these surface measures address the structural, cultural, and historical reality of the police presence in our lives.

To struggling communities, the $8.5 million needed for 14 more cops is more than chump change. It can and should be diverted to the numerous social, housing, nutritional, leadership, and other resilience-supporting programs and initiatives.

While it is necessary to be able to intervene in emergency situations, that task should be transferred to agencies trained to skillfully help people in crisis, not evict, criminalize, or shoot them. We need serious solutions for our serious problems in all their complexity, enlisting the full creative abilities of our communities in the process. We can't just keep pumping money into a paramilitary force that has, in 150 years, never wavered from its founding mission.

Ricardo Levins Morales is an artist and organizer. He lives in Minneapolis.

Police, incarceration don't equal public safety

by Miski Noor (originally appeared in the Star Tribune, 12/3/19)

Nov. 15 marked the fourth anniversary of the night the Minneapolis Police Department murdered Jamar Clark. It was a tragic, heartbreaking moment for the city of Minneapolis, and thousands of us mobilized across the city and country during an 18-day occupation of the Fourth Precinct police station.

I was there and saw how we took care of each other in the face of police standoffs, tear gas and white supremacist violence.

In the years since then, we've continued to build a vision that eradicates violence at the hands of the state. We have held allies, circulated petitions, shut down highways, airports and the Mall of America (twice), passed legislation to protect black lives and over and over again changed the narrative that police equals safety.

Just last year, organizations like the one I build with, Black Visions Collective, as a part of the Reclaim the Block coalition, worked with City Councilmembers Phillipe Cunningham and Steve Fletcher to divert $1 million from the Minneapolis Police Department (MPD) budget into community-led safety initiatives like the Office of Violence Prevention and a race equity coordinator.

Yet organizers envisioning a world where every human life is honored face a charged and dangerous landscape as we try to create the change we so desperately need. Since Jamar Clark was murdered, we have seen the increase in public relations rhetoric from the police, lip service from many elected officials and violence still perpetrated against marginalized communities, especially by those whose role it is to protect our city.

Real shifts in our city have come from community members coming together to define safety for ourselves, block by block, instead of investing in institutions that have always harmed us.

Punishment and incarceration are not solutions. The boom of the prison industrial complex since the 1970s has only served a small group of wealthy men, while the human cost — in destruction of health, families, the environment — has skyrocketed.

Contrary to several Star Tribune editorials supporting additional spending on police (most recently, "Public safety, here and now, in St. Paul," Nov. 27) and incarceration do not create safety.

In fact, they are the arbiters of much of the violence experienced by poor communities of color, trans and gender nonconforming folks, immigrants, sex workers, youth, clergy and many more in our communities.

The appointment of a well-meaning black police chief is a symptom of the misguided approach to reform that Minneapolis is taking. A black chief isn't the answer; fundamentally shifting our city's priorities is.

Chief Medaria Arradondo has asked for 400 new cops — when the city already spends 37% of its general fund on policing and corrections. By comparison, Minneapolis spends only 0.6% of its total budget on jobs programs and 0.2% on youth development programs.

We don't solve racism by appointing black police leaders, but by investing in black communities. Mayor Jacob Frey has included 14 new cops in next year's budget, which forces us to ask: How do you justify the increase of police when we are dedicating so little to jobs programs, youth development and other important community needs?

A budget serves as a statement of our values. By proposing an increase in funding for police, the mayor is communicating the value he places on an archaic and inhumane system of criminalization and violence.

We need our elected representatives to re-imagine what is possible and remember that the community is best equipped to define what safety looks like.

On Trans Day of Remembrance, Nov. 20, we mourned the murders of more than 20 trans folks in 2019. We see uprisings and demands for democracy among people from Iran to Bolivia to right here in Minneapolis. As we mourn, we also must continue to fight for a world in which people's lives and safety are of primary concern to each one of us.

As queer and trans black organizers who have been envisioning a world where we can all be free, we are calling on all of our neighbors to join us in taking control of our imaginations and building a world in which we our communities have the services and support we need, that keep us safe. We deserve a world in which mental health professionals respond to mental health crises, where our youth are not criminalized to satisfy a quota, where conflict transformation and personal transformation are possible.

Such a world is possible. This is an invitation to build it and live in it with us, as it's ours.

Miski Noor is an organizer and writer based in Minneapolis.

Police Shooting of Justine 'Damond' Ruszczyk Exposes a Vicious Double Standard

by Miski Noor (originally appeared in Colorlines, 7/26/17)

Minneapolis Mayor Betsy Hodges has suddenly become interested in police accountability now that media is following the story of Justine Ruszczyk, the White Australian immigrant killed by police on July 16. In the media, the late 32-year-old's lawyer described her as "the most innocent victim ever." One outlet published a video of the meditation instructor saving baby ducklings. And instead of using the common clinical tone to describe Ruszczyk, the headlines almost uniformly identify her as the "bride-to-be."

Aiyana Stanley-Jones was an 8-year-old-to-be.

Trayvon Martin was an 18-year-old-to-be.

Jamar Clark was a 25-year-old-to-be.

The narrative surrounding Ruszczyk, who was fatally shot by Officer Mohamed Noor, is humanizing. She was automatically afforded this grace because she was a White woman killed by state-sanctioned violence.

This is White supremacy.

White supremacy manifests in many ways, including neglecting the lived experiences of oppression that communities of color face, presuming the guilt of victims of color and supposedly progressive politicians who proclaim "Black lives matter" but make dubious alliances.

Over the last week, the nation has watched Minneapolis with anticipation and disbelief, riveted by more fatal police violence unfolding here. Our city has served as one of the major battlegrounds for the sanctity of Black life over the last four years, as Black organizers and activists have pushed to show the world that the Midwest is not only just as racist as the rest of this country, but that this racism is intentional, insidious and often carried out by the very liberals who claim to respect, care for and want to protect Black lives.

In the case of Ruszczyk (who used her fiancée's surname, Damond, professionally) we did not expect accountability from the Minneapolis Police Department. In fact, we saw the city and the police open their usual playbook. The public had to wait more than 12 hours for information about the shooting. And the police were, yet again, investigating themselves, as the Bureau of Criminal Apprehension—the same organization that found Jamar Clark's killers innocent—is leading the investigation into the Ruszczyk killing as well.

It was not until more details emerged about Ruszczyk that this particular case of police violence showed itself to be different from previous ones. Hers is the kind of shooting where much-deserved justice and accountability might be achieved. Not because officials recognize that police violence is a serious problem, but because this system works exactly as it is intended to: to protect Whiteness in general and White womanhood in particular.

The long history of the state protecting the supposed sanctity of White womanhood is one of the primary functions of U.S. institutions, systems and culture. From the violence visited upon Black youth in the name of White womanhood, as in the case of Emmett Till, or in the use of Black women's bodies for surreptitious and dangerous medical experimentation, like in the case of Henrietta Lacks, White woman are protected at the expense of the lives of Black people.

Like other cities in the U.S., poor and young Black women and femme activists in Minneapolis have created space over the years for people to take action, organize their communities and change the material conditions of Black folks. Their work has created a national platform for Minneapolis, but whenever there is a spotlight on our city, politicians co-opt our movement, taking our language and occupying space that was created for change. They push their own agendas, riddled with so-called reforms that don't actually protect or serve our most vulnerable folks.

Case in point: Early this month, during the Minneapolis Democratic-Farmer-Labor Convention, Alondra Cano—a city council candidate that the party endorsed—declared White, male, moneyed, straight mayoral hopeful Jacob Frey to be the "Black lives matter candidate."

When Cano, who is not Black, presumed to speak for any part of The Movement for Black Lives, it illustrated how some progressives devalue the voices and opinions of Black organizers. The co-option, erasure, misinformation and outright lies are harmful to movement work and our communities. This is especially clear because Cano endorsed Frey, someone who reportedly said, "Don't bring those people to my office again," about his own constituents following a Black Lives Matter protest, and who has accepted campaign donations from the Police Officers Federation of Minneapolis.

And this is just one part of the dynamic that plays into the case of Justine Ruszczyk. When I consider the political circumstances surrounding this case, that 53 percent of the nation's White women helped elect President Donald Trump, and that it took the police slaying of a White woman for many in Minneapolis to even consider that the police are a problem, the situation is especially harrowing and painful for Black people who put our bodies on the line for liberation.

It is difficult not to take note of the 7,000 Minneapolis residents who showed up for the impromptu anti-Trump rallies after election day, or the thousands who showed up for the Women's March, but were nowhere to be seen when police used a chemical that was likely pepper spray on 10-year-old Taye Clinton at a protest or when 17-year-old Tania Harris was shot by the police but somehow found herself charged with assault.

While we unequivocally demand justice for every single person harmed by the state, it is astounding to witness the response to Ruszczyk's killing. There have been actions, vigils, marches and rallies almost every day.

(continued)

Mayor Hodges not only condemned the way the police handled the Ruszczyk case, but went as far as to ask Minneapolis Police Chief Janeé Harteau to resign because she'd "lost confidence in the chief's ability to lead us further." In stark juxtaposition, the mayor made no changes after Jamar Clark was killed by the same police department roughly a year and a half ago. Even after police attacked protesters, including a dragging a Black trans youth by their hijab and punching a Black femme in the face, Hodges' response was simply, "I fully support the chief's determination in this case, that Officers Schwarze and Ringgenberg did not violate city policies … I trust the thorough process that the department followed, and I trust Chief Harteau's judgment."

As a part of the local Black Lives Matter chapter and someone who was present when Hodges refused to support the Clark family's request for the release of tapes of the shooting, I know that the difference this time is not a change of heart. Hodges has repeatedly shown a clear disregard for Black life while in office, and forcing Chief Harteau to step down is a politically motivated action of self-preservation that comes as she feels pressure from community members and other mayoral candidates in an election year.

And where are the people who usually advocate for police in these cases? As mainstream media keeps reminding us, Ruszczyk was shot and killed by a Black, Somali, Muslim immigrant police officer, a man whose social identities explain the lack of vocal support in his case. Officer Noor is not being protected in the same ways that Officers Mark Ringgenberg and Dustin Schwarze were after they killed Clark. Harteau told press that, "Justine didn't have to die." I urge her to consider that neither did Clark, just 61 seconds after officers arrived on the 1600 block of Plymouth Ave N.

Media outlets are playing their role as well. Using "Damond" instead of her harder-to-spell and pronounce legal name Ruszczyk ensures that the victim reads as a "real American," despite her recent immigration. This portrayal also creates a more stark contrast to Noor, whose name sounds more foreign, Muslim and Black.

The automatic demonization of Noor is not surprising to Black organizers because hypocritical hashtags like #BlueLivesMatter are intended to protect Whiteness and White supremacy, not individual officers. We have long said that the root of the problem is not individuals, regardless of their race.

The policing system in its entirety targets Black people for death and destruction and we need to replace it with something completely different, something that defunds the police and invests in local initiatives led, executed and evaluated by our communities.

As time moves on and Minneapolis inches closer to election day, we are seeing more and more mayoral and city council candidates use the language of the movement, saying that they wish to see "transformational change." I challenge the candidates to provide their definition of transformational change when it comes to Minneapolis policing and release their plans to reimagine law enforcement in our city. Our lives depend on it.

Miski Noor is an organizer and writer based in Minneapolis.

TACTICAL STATEMENT

1. The purpose of MPD150 is to change the story of policing in Minneapolis in order to set in motion a process for dissolving the Minneapolis Police Department.
2. MPD150 respects that ours is one effort and one approach among many.
3. MPD150 uses research, community dialogue, creative visioning, and cultural activism and encourages widespread community engagement and initiative.
4. MPD150 employs proactive activism, seeking to move beyond reaction. We avoid entrapment in forms of action that undermine our strategy.
5. We oppose any state repression of dissent, including surveillance, infiltration, disruption, and violence against activists or community members.

GUIDING PRINCIPLES

Principles on how we treat each other
- Oppression awareness: Be mindful of how oppression & privilege impact our work and interactions. Recognize & value differences.
- Openness: Be open to offer a different opinion, to ask questions, to pose new ideas, to listen to new ideas, etc.
- Keep end goal in mind: Building strong communities & taking down police state > conflict within group.

Principles on our work structure
- No one owns this: No organization, no person. We are in this space as individuals.
- Decision making: Core group of MPD150 navigates direction of project. Small groups make decisions on their own work with feedback and guidance of core group.
- Confidentiality: Ask group about what you can share; ask an individual if you would like to share something they've said.
- We support each other in many ways through this work, and this work is not a substitute for other therapeutic and healing processes.
- Strategic participation: Know why you're saying what you're saying.
- Acknowledge disagreement, it doesn't have to be an obstacle.
- Let the right process take us to the right work > let the work drive the process
- Follow through: If you can't do something that you committed to, let folks know who will be impacted by this and help delegate the task to someone who can do it.
- Decisions turn into action steps.

A Few Excerpts from MPD150's Timeline Project

The "Enough Is Enough" report contains a brief history of the Minneapolis Police Department, but our researchers found much, much more. What follows is a selection of entries from the *Timeline* section at www.MPD150.com. Find many more there. For these examples, the citation markers are left in; find the notes and links themselves at the website.

IAU, CRA, OPCR: Police (Un)accountability in Minneapolis

"It is a waste of time for anyone to file a complaint against the police."
– Kenneth Brown, former chairman of the Minneapolis Civil Rights Commission, 2012 [1]

When police brutality becomes particularly obvious in Minneapolis, community members often call for increased police accountability. The idea is that with the oversight of civilian review boards, internal affairs units, or other administrative bodies, Minneapolis police officers will stay true to their motto, "to protect with courage and to serve with compassion." Unfortunately, this is almost never the case. From the beginning of MPD's existence in 1887 to the present day, accountability mechanisms have been nearly useless at preventing police misconduct and brutality.

Despite the brutality of MPD in the late nineteenth and early twentieth century toward people of color, the urban poor, and labor organizers, there was no real investigation of civilian complaints against the department until 1963. Until then, the only way to address police brutality was to report it directly to Department management, who was then free to dismiss it without ever making any record of the complaint.

In 1963, a Civil Rights investigation found that "minority group members generally [lacked] faith that their complaints would be dealt with properly,"[2] and recommended the creation of an "impartial police review program with full citizen participation," a recommendation that was mostly ignored by the city—Minneapolis' first Civilian Review Board was created in 1963, but it lacked any official status, and ceased to exist after a lawyer found that its members could be sued for defamation. [3] For most of the 1960s, there continued to be no group investigating police misconduct complaints.

In the late 1960s, the Minneapolis Police Department created the Internal Investigation Unit (now the Internal Affairs Unit, or IAU) to investigate complaints against its own officers, a system widely criticized as ineffective to this day. As a city report put it decades later, "the Internal Affairs Unit has a history of not investigating or thoroughly investigating citizen complaints…officers could not be expected to thoroughly investigate other officers with whom they must later serve."[4] Community members have similar complaints about the IAU today.

In 1967, the City Council, pressured by national and local civil rights organizations, established the Minneapolis Civil Rights Commission [5] to investigate civil rights complaints in Minneapolis. [6] The Commission, staffed by civilians, was given the power to investigate complaints against police officers. Like the first Civilian Review Board, the Civil Rights Commission was largely ineffective; in 1969, after police violently broke up a protest, community organizations and a Star Tribune editorial called for even greater police oversight.[7] Those calls went unheeded.

Meanwhile, the Police Department and the Police Federation fought tooth-and-nail against the commission, refusing to turn over documents, answer questions, or provide testimony in hearings. [8] Eventually, they won: in 1969, the head of the police union, Charles Stenvig, was elected mayor, and in 1971, the Civil Rights Commission's power to investigate police misconduct was revoked by the city. [9] For the next two decades, the only agency empowered to investigate police misconduct would be the police department itself.

Out of 81 complaints of excessive use of force, the IAU didn't find one example of wrongdoing. The Internal Affairs Unit continued to be incredibly ineffective at holding officers accountable through the late 1980s; for example, under the last year of Tony Bouza's tenure as Minneapolis Chief in 1988, 83.6% of the 231 complaints reviewed by the department's internal affairs unit were dismissed with no action whatsoever. Out of 81 complaints of excessive use of force, the IAU didn't find one example of wrongdoing. [10]

By the end of the 1980s, the killing of Lloyd Smalley and Lillian Weiss, along with the brutal arrests of a number of Black youth in an Embassy Suites downtown, led to renewed calls for civilian oversight. In September 1990, a working committee convened by the city recommended the creation of a new oversight group, one that the police would be required to cooperate with. As always, police fought the proposal tooth-and-nail; the Police Federation argued that civilian review would take away officers' right to due process [11], and the department's SWAT team threatened to stop working in protest. [12] The City Council passed the proposal anyway, creating the Civilian Review Authority [13], which had the ability to investigate complaints and issue "findings of fact," but left disciplinary action up to the police chief.

Unsurprisingly, the Civilian Review Authority also failed to hold police accountable. From 1991 to 1996, the CRA resolved 826 complaints, more than 85% of which weren't even fully investigated by the board. Even after investigation, only 6% of complaints were sustained. [14] Five years in, not one officer had ever been fired as a result of a CRA complaint. [15] By nearly all accounts, it never got better; even a police

federation spokesperson once described the CRA as "dysfunctional." [16] Problems with the CRA continued for the next two decades, into the 2010s.

In December 2011, the CRA board issued a public statement declaring that they had no confidence the police chief would impose discipline when they recommended it. [17] In response, the Minneapolis Police Federation, one of the most powerful lobbying groups in the state, pushed the state legislature to pass a law making it illegal for the Civilian Review Authority to issue "findings of fact." It won overwhelming bipartisan support over vehement opposition of Minneapolis' Mayor and City Council, and was signed into law by governor Mark Dayton in the spring of 2012. As Councilmember Cam Gordon said at the time, "I think this effectively forces us to re-evaluate the Civilian Review Authority." [18]

It did. In the fall of 2012, the City Council dismantled the CRA, replacing it with a new oversight agency under the city's Civil Rights Department: the Office of Police Conduct Review, or OPCR, consisting of two civilians and two police officers. The OPCR remains the city's police oversight agency today. Predictably, it has many of the same

issues as its predecessors, with the vast majority of cases being dismissed without any disciplinary action whatsoever. As of August 2017, 1,175 complaints have been filed with the OPCR since its inception, and only 36 have resulted in disciplinary actions other than coaching. In other words, the likelihood of discipline from a complaint is around 3%. [19] And that's only the complaints that are successfully filed. An August 2017 report from the Police Conduct Oversight Commission found that in 13 out of 15 attempts to test-file a complaint at Minneapolis police precincts, people were not given opportunities to file complaints, and information on how to file online was inconsistent. [20]

Since 1963, five separate bodies have been formed to reign in the Minneapolis Police Department. Every single one of these bodies has been weak, unhelpful, and ineffective. When any one of them managed to gain even limited power over police misconduct, the police federation worked successfully to limit their power and destroy them. Our history is clear: real police accountability, civilian review or otherwise, is impossible within our current system.

MPD Under Scrutiny

From 1974 to 1976, independent investigators found the Minneapolis Police Department's treatment of minority groups and its hiring processes unacceptable. A 1974 study of the Twin Cities Native American Community, by the Minnesota Advisory Committee to the US Commission on Civil Rights, found an "unequal application" of the law in Indian and white communities, with minority persons frequently charged with public profanity, or breach of the peace, usually in reaction to insults and abuse from police. In June of 1975, eleven incidents of police brutality that occurred within a short time span led to three public hearings held by the Minnesota State Department of

Human Rights, in conjunction with the Urban League, NAACP and AIM. MPD wasn't thrilled—Captain Wayne Hartley commented that "We are police officers, not Black or Indian or white—and it is prejudiced to talk otherwise." [1]

In 1975, The Minnesota Department of Human Rights issued a probable cause finding of discrimination in the hiring and recruitment of the Minneapolis Police Department. In response, the police department ended the use of a 200-question written screening test that contained math and vocabulary questions (found by the MDHR to be "not job related"). The rookie class in 1975 had 96 hours of Karate and 14 hours

of Transactional Analysis added to their training, with the goal of building the officers' confidence to handle a situation without overreacting. Captain Blanch commented that "basic attitudes are difficult if not impossible to change, but that behavior patterns resulting from those attitudes can be changed through proper training." [2]

But did the reforms work? Were police able to change their racist behavior patterns through proper training? A look at the history of the decades since suggests the answer is no, and that these reforms were just another in a long series of attempts to fix a system that is rotten to its core.

"Trust" as a Four-Letter Word: The PCRC and the PCOC

Part I: The PCRC

The Police Community Relations Council (PCRC) was established in 2003 to build trust between the Minneapolis Police Department and marginalized communities. In the end, it did almost exactly the opposite.

Following MPD's accidental shooting of eleven-year-old Julius Powell and a subsequent riot in the summer of 2002, community members called for a federal mediator from the Department of Justice to help restore police-community trust.[1] When the mediator arrived, an agreement was made between the city and some community members: they would come together as the PCRC for five years, working together to improve police-community relations. MPD was also required to agree to more than 100 action items by the mediation agreement, most of them small departmental reforms.[2]

From the very beginning, there were community members unsure of the usefulness the PCRC, citing the fact that the community representatives were hand-picked by the city council and the lack of Latino/a, Somali, and Southeast Asian representation.[3] They were right to be skeptical: as the initial term of the PCRC wrapped up in 2008, more than 40 of the action items mandated by the mediation agreement were incomplete.[4] The PCRC passed a vote of "no confidence" in the city and asked Mayor Rybak to continue its work for another year, but he refused, and disbanded the PCRC at the end of 2008.

Former members of PCRC asked once more, in 2009, for help from the Department of Justice: this time not for mediation, but to put the Minneapolis Police Department in receivership, forcing it to reform from the top down. The DOJ decided not to get involved this time and, as members of the PCRC said themselves in 2009, their "clarion call for change [remained] unfulfilled, unfunded, and nonexistent."[5]

Part II: The PCOC

Five years after the PCRC was disbanded, Minneapolis decided to give building community-police trust another shot, creating the Police Conduct Oversight Commission (PCOC) in 2013 to audit the newly formed Office of Police Conduct Review (OPCR) and propose potential reforms to the Minneapolis Police Department.[6]

Unfortunately, with no Department of Justice mediation agreement, and no power to force MPD to change, the police are free to adopt whatever PCOC suggestions they like and discard the rest. For example, though the PCOC created a list of policy recommendations for body camera use, it took months of back-and-forth for MPD to add any of them to policy.

One commissioner described it as a "slap in the face," saying that the department's police-community relations strategy was little more than lip service.[7]

If the PCRC and the PCOC are anything to go by, that's what all police-community trust building initiatives are: public relations programs. Increasing "police-community trust" without any real accountability is a losing battle, one that does nothing to keep our city safer from those who are supposed to be protecting us.

The Murder of Fong Lee

On July 22, 2006, nineteen-year-old Fong Lee was with a group of friends outside Cityview elementary school in North Minneapolis when they were attacked by two police officers, Minneapolis officer Jason Andersen and state patrol trooper Craig Benz. The officers, claiming to see a gun changing hands, sped their car across a grassy field, hitting Lee on his bike. [1]

Andersen got out of the squad car, chasing Lee on foot. Claiming that he had a gun and had "raised his arm," Andersen shot him three times in the back, then five more times where he laid on the ground. [2]

From the beginning, there were many inconsistencies with Andersen's description of what happened. Though eyewitnesses reported seeing the squad car hitting Lee's bike, the official police report said that Lee dropped his bike and began running away on foot. [3]

Though law enforcement experts found that no gun was visible in surveillance footage of the incident, Andersen claimed that Lee had a gun, and was pointing it at him. [4]

Andersen also claimed in one account that Lee dropped the gun as he fell to the ground, and in another account that Lee pointed the gun at him from the ground. [5]

There's plenty of evidence to suggest that police planted the gun next to Fong Lee's body. First of all, the gun found next to Lee didn't have his sweat, blood, or fingerprints anywhere on it, and hadn't been fired. [7]

Secondly, the gun that was found next to Lee had been recovered by the Minneapolis Police Department following a burglary two years earlier, and was supposed to be in MPD custody. [8] The officer who had recovered that pistol was the first officer on the scene following the Fong Lee shooting. [9]

Despite all the evidence that Fong Lee didn't do anything wrong, Andersen was returned to duty after only two days, before any investigation had concluded. [11]

He was later cleared of any wrongdoing by an Internal Affairs Investigation and a Hennepin County Grand Jury.

Fong Lee's family also filed a wrongful death lawsuit, but an all-white jury found Andersen not guilty.

Hundreds of community members came together to protest the verdict and demand accountability from the Minneapolis Police Department. [12] The city's response was simple—almost exactly two years after the shooting, the MPD awarded the Medal of Valor, their second-highest honor, to Jason Andersen for killing Fong Lee. [13]

Blaming (and Criminalizing) the Victim: CeCe McDonald

CeCe McDonald, a twenty-three-year-old Black, transgender woman who studied fashion at MCTC, often chose to do her grocery shopping at night.[2] She figured she would be subject to less racism and transphobia at night, when grocery stores are typically less crowded.[3] CeCe went out to do her grocery shopping on the night of June 5, 2011 with some of her friends. On the way, a squad car slowed down to tail them as she walked, finally asking what she was doing out. "We're just going to get some food," a friend answered, and the squad car continued on.

A couple blocks further, CeCe and her friends were passing the Schooner Bar, when several bar patrons outside saw CeCe and started to harass the group, shouting racist and transphobic slurs at them. [4] The verbal insults escalated when someone smashed a glass into the side of CeCe's head with such force that the glass broke, slicing open her face.[5] CeCe, fearing for her life, reached for the only "weapon" she had—a pair of sewing scissors—and stabbed one of her attackers, Dean Schmitz, an avowed white supremacist with a swastika tattoo.[6] Schmitz later died from his injuries.[7] CeCe and her friends retreated to the safety of the nearby Cub parking lot. Someone called 911, and when Minneapolis police arrived, CeCe flagged them down to explain what happened.[8]

After minimal treatment for her injuries from the attack, MPD brought CeCe to City Hall and detained her for three hours before finally questioning her.[9] It was in that state—after being violently attacked, held for hours at the police department, and then interrogated for defending herself against this attack—that the police convinced CeCe to sign a confession of her guilt.[10]

For defending herself in a situation that in so many other cases has ended in the murder of countless trans women of color, CeCe was charged with two accounts of second-degree murder.[11] Her bail was set at $500,000.[12] CeCe was the only person that the MPD arrested that night—not one of her racist, homophobic attackers.[13]

CeCe knew that the deck was stacked against her when her case went to trial, but the judge disallowed key evidence that made a fair outcome impossible. Schmitz' swastika tattoo and known problems controlling his temper weren't allowed into evidence.[14] Neither were CeCe's descriptions of the discrimination and violence that Black trans women face every day. [15] Without this evidence, CeCe knew the jury would never sympathize with a trans Black woman accused of murdering a cis white man, so she accepted a plea deal.[16]

She was sentenced to fort-one months in a men's prison in St. Cloud. [17]

Activists in Minneapolis, Chicago, and around the United States organized solidarity committees to "Free CeCe." [18] Some of her supporters initially called for her to be transferred to a women's prison, but CeCe pushed back against this, saying, "[…]after I did some educating myself on the prison-industrial complex and the history behind African Americans in incarceration, I felt like sending me to any prison wouldn't solve my issue. Men's prisons, women's prisons, they're prisons, and they're not good." [19]

CeCe was released after nineteen months of incarceration, most of it in solitary confinement.[20] Since her release, CeCe has been a leading voice in struggles for racial and gender justice and prison abolition nationally. [21]

CeCe's case is an example of the deep racism and transmisogyny in every facet of our criminal "justice" system, but it is important to remember that her criminalization as a Black trans woman defending her own life started with the Minneapolis Police.

(Find many more timeline entries at www.MPD150.com)

MANUFACTURING CONSENT: A Timeline of Policing and Propaganda

By Devin Hogan

This timeline originally appeared on streets.mn; reprinted here with author's permission, with a handful of design/image changes.

Plymouth Avenue North in July 1967. MNHS via MPD150

1821

The Metropolitan Police Department, the first municipal police force in the world, is created in London. The first American police force forms in Boston 17 years later.

1867

Minneapolis incorporates and the City Council establishes the Minneapolis Police Department, which takes only 36 years to earn the title "The Shame of Minneapolis" due to its legendary corruption and racketeering.

https://www.pbs.org/pov/watch/donotresist/

http://www.minnesotalegalhistoryproject.org/assets/Steffens-%20Shame%20of%20Mpls.pdf

https://en.wikipedia.org/wiki/Bloody_Friday_(Minneapolis)

http://collections.mnhs.org/MNHistoryMagazine/articles/50/v50i03p105-117.pdf

https://en.wikipedia.org/wiki/Minneapolis_general_strike_of_1934

http://minneapolisunions.org/mlr2007-6-21_ahern_full.php

https://www.mnopedia.org/group/aim-patrol-minneapolis

1903

The Citizens' Alliance, a right-wing group representing downtown business interests, forms and spends the next half-century increasingly cementing the Minneapolis Police Department as its personal militia for enforcing anti-labor interests.

1934

Minneapolis police open fire downtown during the Minneapolis General Strike and kill two workers on Bloody Friday. Downtown business interests later invent Aquatennial to overshadow the annual "Teamster Picnics" celebrating the successful strike.

1963

The first Civilian Review Board is established and fails to create meaningful structural change, the same outcome as any other reform-based approach to follow.

1968

Fed up with racist police interactions, community members form the Black Patrol, Soul Force and AIM Patrol to intervene and de-escalate potential violence. After AIM Patrol's first six months, the percentage of the Native population in jail dropped from 70 percent to 10 percent. Community patrols predate the police and continue to this day.

1989

Minneapolis police kill Black elders Lillian Wallace and Lloyd Smalley during a botched SWAT raid, a not-uncommon occurrence that "tarnished" the city's image. Enraged residents, including the current Minnesota Attorney General (image on following page), demand reforms.

1990-1991

In response to a call, Minneapolis police shoot and kill 17-year-old Black resident Tycel Nelson as he is running away. Enraged residents demand reform. **Violent crime peaks in Minneapolis and America and steadily declines for the next three decades without interruption.**

1992-1993

Metro Transit police severely beat an elderly Black man for lack of fare, and furious youth later ambush and kill Minneapolis police officer Jerry Haaf. The Minneapolis Police Department begins terrorizing residents, using tactics including Rough Rides of Native residents, kidnapping, rape, extortion, and opening fire at Little Earth.

2006

In response to a call, Minneapolis police shoot unarmed Black resident Dominic Felder in the back, killing him in the midst of a nervous breakdown. Later that year, Minneapolis police run over 19-year-old Hmong resident Fong Lee on his bicycle and shoot him three times in the back, then shoot another five times more as his body lies on the ground. The officer involved is acquitted.

2007

Five Black Minneapolis police officers—including the current Chief of Police—sue the department for racial discrimination, settling with the city for a record $2 million. The majority of the money is earmarked for (but not required to be spent on) "reform."

2010

In response to a call, Minneapolis police kill 28-year-old Black resident David Smith in the midst of a mental health crisis downtown, suffocating him to death under a prone restraint. Later that year, Hmong resident Jason Yang dies under mysterious circumstances after encountering the Minneapolis police downtown at bar close. **Violent crime in Minneapolis bottoms out and remains at historic lows throughout the decade.**

2013

In response to a call, Minneapolis police corner unarmed 22-year-old Black resident Terrance Franklin in a Lyn-Lake basement, then shoot and kill him. An hour later, Minneapolis police run over and kill resident Ivan Romero in the intersection of 26th and Blaisdell while on the way to the scene. The then-new Chief of Police, who had previously sued the department for sex discrimination, says reform is coming.

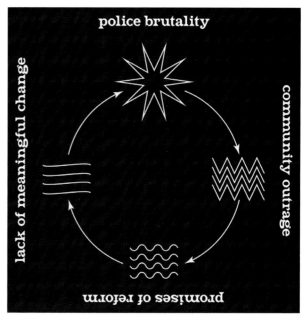

Image: Elin Miller | IG: @elinmiller

KEITH ELLISON ADDRESSES DEMONSTRATORS RESPONDING TO POLICE BRUTALITY IN MINNEAPOLIS.

https://time.com/4779112/police-history-origins/

https://www.nytimes.com/2019/02/03/nyregion/muslim-community-patrol-brooklyn.html

https://www.twincities.com/2007/12/17/botched-police-raids-not-so-rare/

https://www.apnews.com/962eed0dea6d4ccdadbbe151564b7413

https://www.latimes.com/archives/la-xpm-1991-02-12-mn-1357-story.html

http://www.startribune.com/minnesota-police-officers-convicted-of-serious-crimes-still-on-the-job/437687453/

https://www.mprnews.org/story/2010/10/25/excessive-force-verdict

https://www.mprnews.org/story/2009/05/28/fong-lees-family-angered-by-verdict

https://www.twincities.com/2009/01/10/ruben-rosario-cops-off-duty-club-questioned-in-lawsuit/

https://www.twincities.com/2010/11/23/family-officials-at-odds-over-claim-man-was-shot-while-fleeing-minneapolis-police-2/

2014

#Pointergate becomes the first baseless local performative law-and-order outrage in the new Black Lives Matter era. Glen Taylor, a North Mankato-based downtown Minneapolis sports billionaire, purchases the local paper of record, promising a deliberate rightward lurch over time.

2015

Minneapolis police kill 24-year-old Black resident Jamar Clark, shooting him in the face in response to an ambulance call. Residents occupy the nearby Fourth Precinct for the next 18 days to protest and build community, during which the Minneapolis police point assault weapons in the faces of current and future City Council members.

2017

In response to a call, Minneapolis police shoot and kill 40-year-old white resident and Australian national Justine Ruszczyk Damond, sparking international outrage.

2018

In response to a call, Minneapolis police shoot and kill 31-year-old Black resident Thurman Blevins as he is running away. Six months later, Minneapolis police shoot and kill 36-year-old Black resident Travis Jordan in his front yard during a welfare check. Three weeks later, the City Council votes down the mayor's request to increase the police budget by $12 million annually, choosing instead to invest in upstream safety measures.

Mayor Betsy Hodges points at a resident while posing for a picture during a Get Out the Vote doorknock, the basis of #Pointergate. It is not the first time the mayor has pointed at a resident while posing for a picture.

2019

March

• **Thursday, March 7, 5:52 p.m.**
Cutting police budgets is not the way toward equitable communities
By Editorial Board
Statistics show that cutting police budgets is likely to backfire on cities.

— nota bene [n.b.] statistics quite clearly show the opposite

• **Tuesday, March 12, 10:26 p.m.**
Minneapolis police chief reiterates desire for department to grow to 1,000 officers, despite resistance The issue of understaffing resurfaced at a public meeting in the Cedar Riverside neighborhood last week.

— n.b. the article states the police can't even fill current openings, let alone an expanded force. Where, exactly, does that extra money go?

http://www.citypages.com/news/meet-the-people-of-the-fourth-precinct-occupation-7846325

https://twitter.com/lisabendermpls/status/667496902452088832

https://www.chicagotribune.com/nation-world/ct-minnesota-police-shooting-jamar-clark-protest-20151119-story.html

https://www.washingtonpost.com/news/morning-mix/wp/2018/07/30/thurman-blevins-shooting-graphic-body-cam-footage-shows-fleeing-black-man-killed-by-minneapolis-police-who-say-he-was-armed/

http://www.startribune.com/minneapolis-council-trims-police-budget-increase-to-fund-anti-violence-efforts/501681431/

https://www.usatoday.com/story/news/investigations/2019/02/13/marshall-project-more-cops-dont-mean-less-crime-experts-say/2818056002/

https://www.washingtonpost.com/news/the-watch/wp/2017/02/14/a-day-with-killology-police-trainer-dave-grossman/

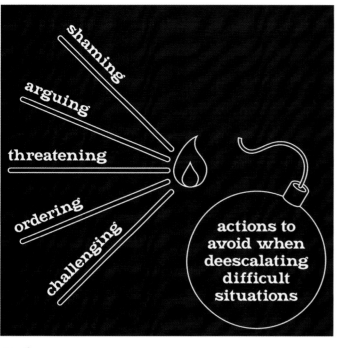

Image: Elin Miller | IG: @elinmiller

April

• **Friday, April 12, 6:38 p.m.**
Counterpoint: Adding cops could satisfy seemingly different interests
By Steve Cramer
The case for a larger force lies in better, not more policing. That could help strengthen communities and police-community relations.

— n.b. four months later this author, a private citizen, singlehandedly closed off a public sculpture downtown with no public input or approval, nor any penalty or recourse for doing so

• **Thursday, April 18, 10:35 p.m.**
Minneapolis to ban 'warrior' training for police, Mayor Jacob Frey says (Mayor Jacob Frey made the announcement in his State of the City address).

• **Wednesday, April 24, 9:28 p.m.**
Minneapolis police union offers free 'warrior' training, in defiance of mayor's ban (Police federation says the Minneapolis mayor's ban on training is illegal).

• **Thursday, April 25, 6:07 p.m.**
Editorial counterpoint: Not well-named, maybe, but 'Warrior Training' is highly valuable
By Richard Greelis
Friendly cop-citizen contacts are the routine. This training simply instills a cautious, resolute mind-set in case the next encounter isn't.

— n.b. as Radley Balko wrote in the Washington Post, the goal of Bulletproof Warrior Training is "teaching cops how to escalate, how to see the world as their enemy and how to find the courage to kill more people, more often"

May

• **Friday, May 10, 9:39 p.m.**
Minneapolis taxpayers will feel effect of record $20 million settlement
Mpls. has reserves to pay Damond settlement, but property taxes might rise

• **Wednesday, May 29, 10:01 p.m.**
Minneapolis police 'behind the ball' on years-old Department of Justice report
Department was advised to alter discipline policies.

— tl;dr the police continue their century-long unreformable streak, even when the federal government gets involved

July

• **Friday, July 5, 5:52 p.m.**
Helping downtown Minneapolis survive and thrive
By Editorial Board
Minneapolis is better because of a decade of work by DID ambassadors.

— tl;dr the Editorial Board disparages the city for repealing spitting and lurking laws, then extols the visible success and virtue of safety beyond policing downtown via DID, demanding the city invest more in these methods

• **Monday, July 8, 7:34 p.m.**
Calls for more cops grow as authorities ID man fatally shot in downtown Minneapolis
Shakopee man is third homicide victim since Memorial Day weekend in downtown Mpls.

— tl;dr who is calling for more cops? Two white men, Steve Cramer and Joe Tamburino, whose ideas the chief public defender of Hennepin County calls "unconstitutional" in the article

• **Wednesday, July 17, 6:44 p.m.**
Another downtown Minneapolis shooting puts spotlight on security plans
By Editorial Board
Gunfire at Crave underscores need for businesses to work with city and police.

July (continued)

• **Thursday, July 18, 4:55 a.m.**
Minneapolis chief wants to add 400 street cops by 2025
Arradondo cites increased pressure and workload.

— n.b. "police per capita" referenced in the article is self-justifying hokum. During the 1950s the entire department had well under 700 people when 100,000 more people lived in Minneapolis

• **Friday, July 26, 12:09 p.m.**
Minneapolis needs more patrol officers, but chief's request to add 400 is too high
By Editorial Board
Medaria Arradondo's recent proposal would raise the total Police Department complement to at least 1,300 by 2025.

— tl;dr the Editorial Board, none of whom live in Minneapolis, repeat the assertion that "business leaders" (Steve Cramer and Joe "unconstitutional" Tamburino) want more cops

• **Sunday, July 28, 5:38 p.m.**
In Minneapolis, 911 nonresponses underscore needs for more cops, advocates say
Mpls. chief sees "critical" officer shortage; others say more cops not answer.

— tl;dr others include Council Member Andrew Johnson, who sensibly points out Minneapolis is one of the only cities nationwide to dispatch two officers to every single call

• **Tuesday, July 30, 8:01 p.m.**
Minneapolis Mayor Jacob Frey faces off against City Council on call for more police
Several council members have spoken out against it.

— tl;dr adding 400 officers will cost at least $45 million per year

• **Tuesday, July 30, 10:23 p.m.**
Minneapolis officials say they undercounted delayed police responses by 5,525 calls
The mix-up was attributed to confusion about the way some of the calls were coded.

— n.b. the article notes "the number of delayed-response calls decreased about 5%, from 7,188 over the previous 12 months," despite no new sworn officers

July (continued)

• **Wednesday, July 31, 5:38 p.m.**
Readers Write: Delayed 911 responses
By Jeanne Torma
Minneapolis' slow 911 response rate is jaw-dropping.

— tl;dr "Police officers don't usually prevent crime; they respond to it"

August

• **Friday, August 2, 10:40 a.m.**
Minneapolis police chief promises 'transformational' change as staffing debate continues
He eyes "transformational" policies, as police staffing complicates budget talks.

— n.b. 150 years of history show there is no such thing as transformational reform

• **Friday, August 2, 6:06 p.m.**
Crime laws didn't form in a vacuum — as I can attes
By D.J. Tice
Now-detested policies were a response, people seem to forget.

— tl;dr amid "bipartisan" cries against "systemic racism," the columnist from Arden Hills—himself the victim of serious crimes 40 years ago—reminds us the era of mass incarceration happened for a reason.

• **Friday, August 2, 10:03 p.m.**
Minneapolis police shoot, kill man at apparent domestic call
Officials said that the man shot a woman, who is expected to survive.

• **Wednesday, August 7, 9:45 p.m.**
Two officers in north Minneapolis Christmas tree controversy have been fired
The officers were put on administrative leave shortly after a photo of the tree surfaced on social media. The police union is appealing the firings.

— n.b. the entire proverb is "A few bad apples spoil the barrel"

https://andrewjohnsonmpls.tumblr.com/post/186401877011/an-alternative-to-adding-400-additional-patrol

https://www.nytimes.com/2019/09/26/opinion/the-police-cant-solve-the-problem-they-are-th problem.html

FOX NEWS channel
► LT. BOB KROLL | PRESIDENT, MPD FEDERATION
MINNEAPOLIS MAYOR GOES HEAD TO HEAD WITH POLICE OVER MANDATORY PLACARDS AIMED AT HELPING ILLEGALS

August (continued)

• Thursday, August 8, 9:00 p.m.
Minneapolis reaches tentative $200,000 settlement with family of Jamar Clark
Lawyer says they realized change would not come via courts; Mpls. must approve deal.

• Friday, August 16, 11:12 a.m.
Minneapolis mayor requests 14 more cops in next year's budget
Mayor Jacob Frey's 2020 budget includes response to police chief's plea.

— tl;dr while being shouted down by members of Jamar Clark's family, the mayor invokes the name of Jerry Haaf before proposing new beat cops and officers to clear old sexual assault cases, none of which relate to delayed 911 responses

• Friday, August 16, 5:59 p.m.
Twin Cities mayors face difficult realities of urban growth
By Editorial Board
Both Minneapolis and St. Paul are growing, but so are concerns about public safety and city services.

— n.b. whose concerns are growing? The Editorial Board doesn't say

• Tuesday, August 27, 10:05 p.m.
Minneapolis police mounted patrol mourns loss of 'kind, gentle' steed
The 20-year-old buckskin gelding was put down after suffering a serious leg injury on Sunday.

— tl;dr "The life of a police horse is one of hours spent entertaining children at parades, block parties and other events — punctuated by moments of intensity"

September

• Friday, September 6, 5:38 p.m.
Majority of Minneapolis residents back hiring more patrol officers
By Editorial Board
Citywide survey shows strong support for adding officers to the overburdened force.

— n.b. the survey in question is a push poll paid for by the Downtown Council (Steve Cramer) and Chamber of Commerce, who did not release responses for every question, including the majority who said structural reform is needed before spending more money on police

• Friday, September 6, 9:29 p.m.
Lawsuit alleges Minneapolis police shot service dogs, then tried to cover it up
The 2017 incident went viral after owner posted a video of the encounter. The city attorney says they are reviewing the lawsuit before commenting.

• Thursday, September 12, 5:33 p.m.
Editorial counterpoint: Minneapolis residents have mixed views on policing
By Steve Fletcher
A desire for adding officers is tempered by concerns over how the Police Department operates.

— tl;dr "The department is struggling to manage the flow of retirements; parental, medical, and military leaves; suspensions; and other forms of short-term attrition. If too many of these happen in one precinct on one shift, it puts significant strain on our system, and Minneapolis residents feel it."

• Thursday, September 12, 9:55 p.m.
Minneapolis City Council warms to request for more police officers
Mayor Jacob Frey wants 14 new officers; some council members now call for even more.

— tl;dr "The new positions, among other department requests, would raise the department's budget for next year by $8.5 million to $193.4 million — about 12% of the total city budget."

https://andrewjohnsonmpls.tumblr.com/post/186401877011/an-alternative-to-adding-400-additional-patrol

https://www.nytimes.com/2019/09/26/opinion/the-police-cant-solve-the-problem-they-are-the-problem.html

September (continued)

• Friday, September 13, 10:06 p.m.
How safe is downtown Minneapolis? Police stats validate perception of rising crime
Police officials say crime statistics back up the view that safety has deteriorated in the city's business center.

— tl;dr there have been 28 shootings downtown, up from the five-year historical average of 27 over the same time period

• Monday, September 16, 5:38 p.m.
Readers Write: Downtown Minneapolis crime
By Garth Thoresen
How safe is Minneapolis? Not very.

— tl;dr the author, who lives in Eagan, bemoans "despicable acts of thugs on full display across the nation," calling the family members of those slain by Minneapolis police "professional agitators"

• Tuesday, September 24, 5:47 p.m.
City leaders must act to keep downtown Minneapolis safe
By Lester Bagley, Matt Hoy and Ted Johnson
We want our professional sports teams proud to welcome fans downtown.

— tl;dr representatives of local sports billionaires, citing the Chamber's push poll, have no new ideas

• Saturday, September 28, 9:56 p.m.
Sack Cartoon: Welcome to the Twin Cities
By Steve Sack (cartoon depicts a "welcome to the twin cities sign plus rental racks for bikes, scooters, and kevlar vests)

• Sunday, September 29, 10:48 p.m.
Two fatal shootings over weekend in Twin Cities spark unease | St. Paul nears record for number of slayings.

— tl;dr people looking to party downtown are having second thoughts

• Monday, September 30, 8:50 p.m.
Tied to Trump rally? Police union sees partisanship in ban on uniformed cops backing candidates
Mpls. union leader says policy is aimed at the force's Trump supporters.

— n.b. over 90% of Minneapolis police officers do not live in Minneapolis

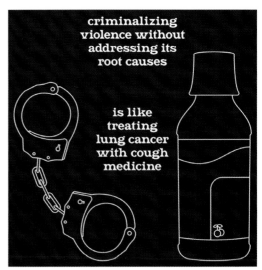

Image: Elin Miller | IG: @elinmiller

October

• Wednesday, October 2, 7:30 p.m.
AP-NORC poll: Most say whites treated more fairly by police

— tl;dr "About 7 in 10 black Americans, and about half of Hispanics, call police violence against the public very serious, compared with about a quarter of white Americans."

• Wednesday, October 2, 9:36 p.m.
Minneapolis Park Board votes to offer settlement to Somali teens handcuffed at a city park

• Wednesday, October 2, 10:04 p.m.
FBI: Violent crime in Minnesota dropped last year, continuing decadelong trend
The Twin Cities area remains one of the safest metros in America, according to FBI data.

• Thursday, October 3, 12:24 p.m.
Business leaders call for more police in downtown Minneapolis
City Council Member Lisa Goodman joined them and said she would like to hire more officers and rethink other policies to improve safety in the area.

— tl;dr Steve Cramer held a press conference. "More than 630 violent crimes have taken place downtown so far this year, almost 100 more than the same time last year but 120 fewer than 2017, according to data from the Minneapolis Police Department."

https://twitter.com/dbrauer/status/1171128223142268928?ref_src=twsrc%5Etfw

https://www.minnpost.com/politics-policy/2014/12/94-percent-minneapolis-police-officers-live-outside-city-minneapolis-does-it/

• Friday, October 4, 7:32 p.m.
Minneapolis North Siders air concerns about troubled street corner
N. 21st and Aldrich has been plagued by drugs, shootings and violence.

— tl;dr "These aren't robots, these aren't people who are unreachable, but we can't be afraid to approach these guys," said Pastor Edrin Williams of Sanctuary Covenant Church.

• Monday, October 7, 11:14 a.m.
Twin Cities property tax hikes take biggest bite in less wealthy areas
Mpls., St. Paul proposals could bring 15% increase to some poorer areas.

— n.b. the police are the third-most expensive budget item after Public Works and Capital Improvement

• Monday, October 7, 2:07 p.m.
Minneapolis police union selling "Cops for Trump" T-shirts, in wake of uniform ban
Mpls. police say the move was in the works before Trump announced visit.

• Monday, October 7, 10:47 p.m.
Detention sought for young repeat Minneapolis offenders
Policy change meant to address Mpls. crime wave.

— tl;dr perception of increased crime downtown is tied to one specific group. Minors from the group are diverted from jail to the Juvenile Supervision Center, where some 10 percent to 13 percent walk out after waiting up to 10 hours to be offered shelter or a guardian. Because the jail has significantly more resources than diversion programs, repeat offenders will be sent to jail instead.

Image: An artist (not affiliated with MPD150) made these signs/stickers and put them up around the Twin Cities a few months before the MPD150 report launch in November 2017.

COMMUNITY POLICING AND OTHER FAIRY TALES

Between 2019 and 2020, writers and artists, mostly based here in Minneapolis, worked together to create this comic book addressing and dispelling common myths about police and policing. The full comic book is included here, and is also available as a standalone document (both digital and physical); find more at www.MPD150.com.

COMMUNITY POLICING
- AND -
OTHER FAIRY TALES

Pull-Out Poster inside!

COMICS & STORIES FOR A POLICE-FREE WORLD

JONAS GOONFACE • MYC DAZZLE • DENNIS MADAMBA • FERRAYA
MOLLIE W • RICARDO LEVINS MORALES • MICAH BAZANT • MPD150.COM

COMMUNITY POLICING AND OTHER FAIRY TALES

A COLLECTION OF COMICS & STORIES FOR A POLICE-FREE WORLD, CURATED BY MPD150

INSIDE:

AN ORDINARY DAY • MYC DAZZLE

SWEET TEAMS & S.W.A.T. TEAMS - A HISTORY OF COMMUNITY POLICING • DENNIS MADAMBA

SPEAKING UP ABOUT STINGS • MOLLIE W & FERRAYA

WHY IS THERE A COP ROAMING THRU OUR HALLS? • JONAS GOONFACE & YOUNG PEOPLE'S ACTION COALITION

PULLOUT POSTER BY **MICAH BIZANT**

ADDITIONAL ART BY **RICARDO LEVINS MORALES**

SUPPLEMENTAL WORDS & RESOURCES FROM **MPD150**

First printing Minneapolis, MN (Occupied Dakota territory), June 2020
PDF download available at MPD150.com

UNAPPROVED BY THE COMICS CODE AUTHORITY

An Ordinary Day

written and illustrated by @MycDazzle
story inspired by Malcolm Jamison

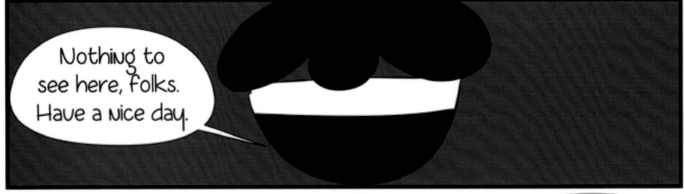

SWEET TEAMS

& S.W.A.T. TEAMS

DENNIS MADAMBA

A HISTORY OF COMMUNITY POLICING

COMMUNITY POLICING IS ABOUT DEVELOPING PERSONAL RELATIONSHIPS WITH COPS-- VIA POLICE/ YOUTH SPORTS AND SOCIAL ACTIVITIES, COPS ON BIKES, VISIBLE ACTS OF CHARITY, PRECINCT OPEN HOUSES AND "OFFICER FRIENDLY" VISITS TO CLASSROOMS.

NATIONAL NIGHT OUT

BACK IN THE 1960S, WE HAD TO TAKE CARE OF A LOT OF PROTEST MOVEMENTS.

WE DEMAND DECENT HOUSING NOW!

WE DEMAND EQUALITY!

WE DEMAND EQUALITY!

WE DEMAND EQUALITY!

WE DEMAND DECENT HOUSING NOW!

WE DEMAND EQUAL RIGHTS NOW!

NOW!

IT DIDN'T MAKE US VERY POPULAR.

MORE ICE CREAM

COMMUNITY CONTACTS

THE RESULT (AND THE MAIN GOAL) IS A STEADY INFLOW OF INFORMATION TO THE POLICE. THE "INFORMATION SHARING" BETWEEN POLICE AND COMMUNITY FLOWS IN ONLY ONE DIRECTION.

WARNING

NEIGHBORHOOD WATCH
WE REPORT ALL SUSPICIOUS ACTIVITIES TO OUR POLICE DEPARTMENT

COMMUNITY MEETINGS

ANOTHER TOOL IN OUR BELT!

In the physical version of the comic, this image (by Micah Bizant) is a pull-out poster.

Every year the Minneapolis Police Department approaches the City Council for more money.

In June 2018, the Minneapolis Police Department announced that it would end its marijuana stings, after it was revealed that 46 of the 47 people charged with felonies were black.

"Officers have directly asked black men to facilitate drug deals with other black men, and have then requested that the facilitator be charged with sale...Officers are seeking out extremely low-level marijuana transactions with people of color and are then arresting and booking the sellers and submitting the cases for felony charging."
--County Public Defender

Minneapolis Police Dept to Halt Racially Targeted Cannabis Stings

That stuff is just so messed up, right??

What stuff?

Those targeted cannabis stings.

Minneapolis Police Dept to Halt Racially Targeted Cannabis Stings

MPD set to end a series of undercover cannabis stings after it was revealed that 46 of the 47 individuals who were charged with felonies are black.

I mean, if you're going to be selling drugs in public, shouldn't you be taken off the streets?

Who are we calling dangerous in public? Cops literally kill people in broad daylight- criminalizing just isolates drug users and fills up prisons.

Weed isn't even illegal in like eleven states, but MPD has this as a top priority for some reason?

Those resources could have gone to actually treating drug addiction.

But the whole point of this?

Just setting these people up,

and then punishing them.

White sports fans can get wasted in public and light cars on fire, and cops won't even arrest or charge them.

Well yeah, but if someone is doing drugs in public...

Those white kids across the street are literally hitting a pen right now, you don't think that's a problem?

Uhh....

It's a double standard.

Sixteen of the people in those Minneapolis Police Department marijuana stings had already been convicted and the County Attorney made no effort to expunge the charges.

Cops do not make people safer. In the case of these stings, cops specifically targeted black people on Hennepin Avenue, asking if anyone had any weed. In the case of Jacob Aikens, he was immediately surrounded by four cops after making the sale to an undercover cop.

At this same time in June of 2018, the City of Minneapolis released a report detailing instances in which MPD pressured Emergency Medical Services to sedate patients. Cops caught on bodycam were referring to the sedative, Ketamine, as "the good stuff." One officer, after EMS double-dosed a patient, exclaimed jokingly, "he just hit the k-hole."

This report stated that when EMS and the police co-respond, cops quickly begin calling the shots on the scene, demanding that EMS enact abusive practices such as forcibly sedating patients with a drug that's also used as a date rape drug and a horse tranquilizer.

Imagine a world where there are no cops pressuring EMS. Where medics facilitate patient-driven decisions.

These same communities targeted with forcible sedation also hold sacred, ancestral knowledge about healing the body. There are so many possibilities in a police-free future.

Minneapolis Police Dept to
Racially Targeted Cannabis S

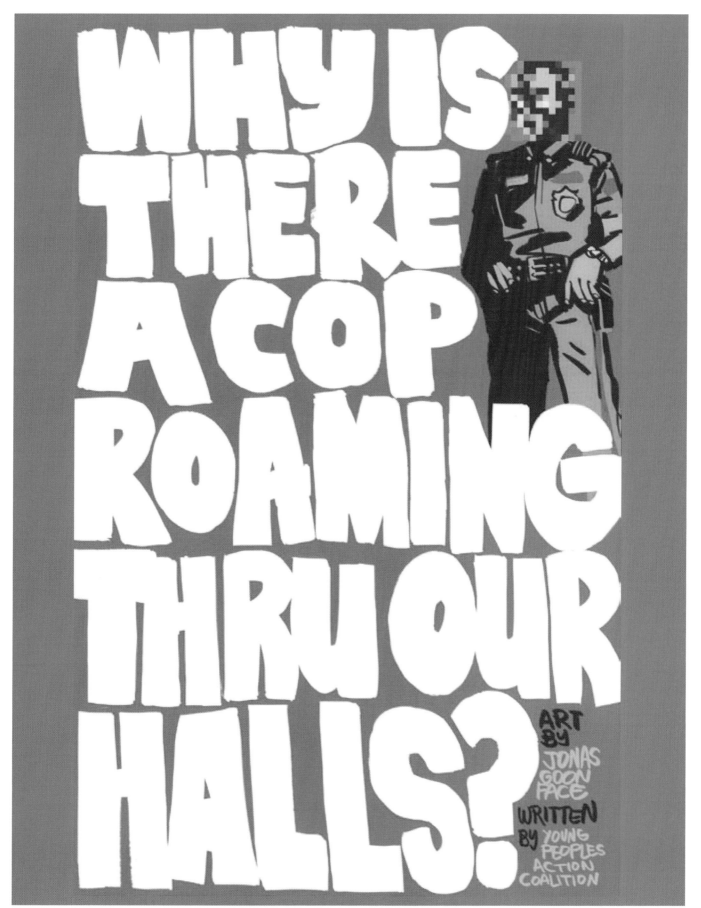

WHY IS THERE A COP ROAMING THRU OUR HALLS?

ART BY JONAS GOON FACE

WRITTEN BY YOUNG PEOPLES ACTION COALITION

Okay but who would protect the school?

We usually have backup cops from outside the school get called anyway if something does happen.

Personally I don't like cops and it'll always be *fuck12*...

...but the SRO is the basketball and football coach on our teams and I think he's cool.

I'm glad he's nice to a bunch of kids in the school, but howabout other SRO's in other schools.

Some of these officers are not the nicest or the most professional.

Has anyone heard about the SRO at *Central High School?*

123

SHAYA 1:26PM

I'm not good
It really
hurts thinking
about it.

SEEN

Kasey.

it'll be okay. You know
I'm always here for you
if you wanna talk
about anything.

Thank you Kasey 🖤

Listen right we were in
class talking about the
SRO in our school but I
don't know if they're
good or not.

I NEED HELP!

TAP

Don't worry
about it.
I gotchu|

TAP TAP

come to this Young People's
Action Coalition meeting
tonight at 6:30

We having a chill meeting
so it'll be fun!

Word okay merch
I'll b there!

SEEN

NO COPS IN SCHOOL

YPAC (YOUNG PEOPLES ACTION COALITION) HAS BEEN WORKING FOR A NUMBER OF YEARS ON GATHERING INPUT FROM YOUTH ON HOW THEY FEEL ABOUT SROS (SCHOOL RESOURCE OFFICERS) AND ENGAGING STUDENTS FROM ACROSS THE METRO IN DIALOGUE AND ACTION ON THE ISSUE OF COPS IN SCHOOLS. THIS COMIC REFLECTS CONVERSATIONS STUDENTS HAVE HAD WITH THEIR PEERS AND SOME OF THE VIOLENCE AND TENSION THAT HAS RESULTED FROM HAVING COPS IN SCHOOLS. IF YOU ARE A MINNEAPOLIS HIGH-SCHOOL STUDENT AND YOU ARE INTERESTED IN OUR WORK, SEND US A MESSAGE ON INSTAGRAM (YPAC.MN) OR FACEBOOK, OR COME TO A MEETING!

THIS COMIC WAS MADE IN COLLABORATION BETWEEN YPAC, MPD150, AND COMIC ARTIST JONAS GOONFACE. THE SCRIPT WAS COLLECTIVELY PUT TOGETHER BY MINNEAPOLIS HIGHSCHOOL STUDENTS AND ABDOULIE CEESAY, A RECENT GRADUATE FROM SOUTHWEST HIGH SCHOOL AND YPAC FACILITATOR. IF YOU ARE INTERESTED IN SUPPORTING OUR WORK, YOU CAN SEND US DONATIONS VIA VENMO @WHYPAAK.

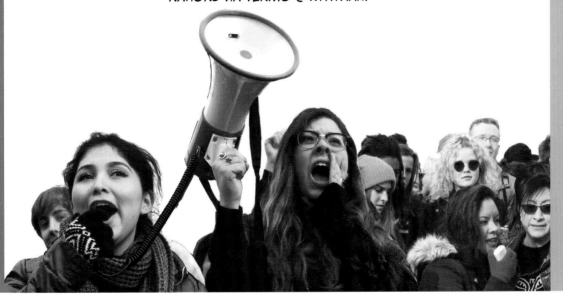

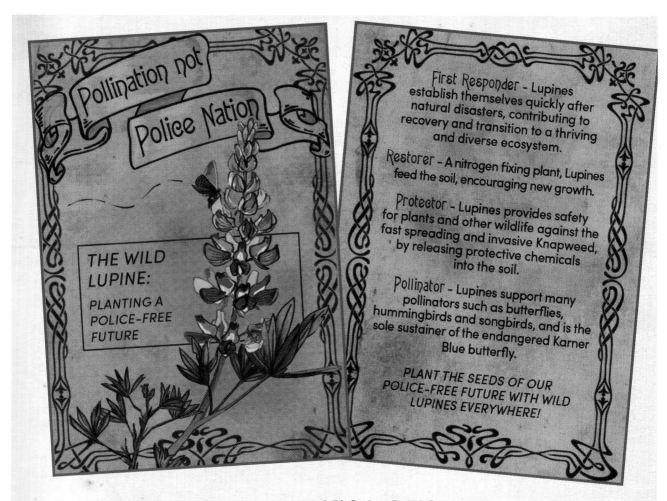

THE PERENNIAL **WILD LUPINE** IS THE
OFFICIAL POLICE ABOLITION FLOWER OF MINNESOTA.

WITH MANY PRACTICAL AND SYMBOLIC PARALLELS TO THE CULTIVATION OF A POLICE-FREE FUTURE, **WILD LUPINE** IS RECOMMENDED FOR PUBLIC SEEDING IN YARDS, GARDENS, EMPTY LOTS, ROADSIDES AND NEAR POLICE STATIONS AND PRISONS. PLANT THE MESSAGE OF THE POLLI-NATION WE WILL BRING TO LIFE.

FOR DETAILS ON ORDERING AND CULTIVATION VISIT:
MPD150.COM

THE WILD LUPINE WAS CHOSEN FOR ITS PROPERTIES AND SYMBOLISM AND AS A NATIVE PLANT IN MINNESOTA. OTHER REGIONS WISHING TO SEED THE FUTURE SHOULD RESEARCH NATIVE PLANT SPECIES FOR THEIR AREA.

POLLINATION, NOT POLICE NATION:

An Oral History of the MPD150 Project

What follows are a few questions about the MPD150 project, along with responses from a number of the core members of the collective.

It's important to note that the report and subsequent followup projects were very much collective efforts, involving the work of dozens of writers, activists, artists, designers, and supporters, over the course of four years.

Not everyone who was involved was able to share their thoughts here, and some have chosen to remain anonymous. We're endlessly grateful to everyone who helped make this work possible, in large and small ways, in public and in private.

An ongoing theme in the responses here is that the MPD150 project was not driven by ego or a desire for credit. We did, however, feel that it was important to tell the story of this work, *especially if that story can be useful to organizers in other communities looking to do similar projects.*

ORIGIN STORIES:

How did you get involved, and what drew you to the project?

RICARDO: The possibility of a project like this came to me while having a conversation with Molly, who would be among the first core members and would later organize our exhibit. I was looking at the wall and noticed on one of my posters (made during the protests of Jamar Clark's murder) a description of the MPD "protecting wealth and whiteness since 1867."

It made me wonder if there was an organizing opportunity here. What if we could take control of the anniversary to tell a people's history of the police and offer a bigger vision for activism than the tepid reforms that kept coming up as demands?

ARIANNA: I was one of the first onboard with Ricardo. There was the infamous email that he sent out to a handful of folks that was just "I have a project I want to tell you about, gonna be big, when can you meet?" I thought: there's just very little information in there, and the less information, the more interesting it's going to be with him, so of course I'm going to go.

I was a young organizer who was unbelievably burnt out by what was going on in the organizing community at the time, and in the political community nationally; there weren't really sustainable models of changemaking out there. Folks were dropping like flies, and was one of them; I was ready to quit. Ricardo had also, through a lot of other conversations, been talking about not doing anything that isn't life-giving...

...the work shouldn't kill you. So he and I met and he ended up just telling me that next year was the 150th anniversary of the Minneapolis Police Department and nobody seemed to realize that. So we started talking more about what a public history project could be. And I think this is something he pulled me in on because a lot of the work I do is really narrative-based; everything I do is to help people tell their own stories. We've always known what we needed, we've always known our own stories.

But it was that damn email!

NIKKI: I was doing a lot of direct action planning and organizing in the Twin Cities in response to police brutality and the murders of Jamar Clark and Philando Castile. I was drawn to this particular project because of the visioning emphasis that seemed more proactive and long-term. It looked like it'd be more about strategic thinking than responding to crises as they come up.

TONY: I was invited to join MPD150 as a paid report writer in June 2017. Multiple members had seen the abolitionist work that I had done as an organizer at Neighborhoods Organizing for Change, and thought I would be a good fit to help coordinate the report writing project.

I had an interview with a few members of the core team, and it seemed like a great project and a great job, so I decided to get involved. I had met many of the organizers working on the project over the years, but didn't have close relationships with many of them. The opportunity to get to know and learn from a huge variety of movement folks was definitely an added incentive to get involved.

I had just come from an organization very focused on turnout and public displays of power, which often felt exhausting and crisis-driven. The opportunity to try and create some resources that would shift the narrative was exciting, particularly given how much I love writing. I'm also a history nut, and had always been curious about the history of the department, especially of murders by the department. The opportunity to delve deep and excavate old stories was very exciting. Finally, I'll just note that I was broke! When MPD150 brought me on, it was well-paid and interesting work on my own terms, something I desperately needed.

KYLE: I got involved wholly because of relationships. Police abolition, though something I supported in the abstract, was not an issue I saw myself diving headfirst into. So I got drawn into MPD150 first just because I happened to know Ricardo and Tony. I stayed with this work, though, because I found something extremely energizing and powerful about this kind of visionary, narrative-driven organizing.

YENTHI: I got involved through my partner, a few months before the report was launched. There was a lot of energy and excitement in helping people in our community understand the history of policing in our city, and seeing that a police-free world is not only possible, but necessary.

MARTIN: I got involved somewhere after the start but before the report was fully written. My longtime friend Tony was working for and with the group on the writing process, and reached out asking if I'd be interested in helping keep track of the financials for the project. Over time, I ended up coming to core group meetings and being more involved for a good portion of the project.

I suppose what initially drew me to the idea, other than the involvement of people I trusted, was the idea of doing work that was both hopeful and imaginative. Particularly around issues of policing, a lot of the work we end up having to do is reactionary and crisis-driven, so the opportunity to do something that not only imagined a better world, but provided concrete steps for working towards it, seemed like a breath of fresh air.

JAE HYUN: I came onto the team after the report had been released, in the run up to the exhibit in 2018. I heard Ricardo speak about it at the Abolish Border Imperialism convening as part of the keynote panel and it's the first time I remember someone putting the phrase "police abolition" in front of me. It instantly clicked as something I want for our community and as something that I have gotten to experience.

I've been fortunate to live in a few different countries and have experienced policing/enforcement through different cultural lenses as well as through the different kinds of documentation I've held or been perceived to hold. I've been able to see firsthand that safety in communities takes different forms and has existed without formalized policing for generations. I wanted to be part of that conversation as it continued to build in our city and left info to volunteer on the MPD150 website to get connected.

SHEILA: Tony was the first person who brought me into the project in late summer 2017. We actually first worked together in a restaurant years before, and I had worked on some city budget "safety beyond policing" work with Tony in 2016, and I was looking for a way to get into organizing. I was pretty new to organizing, and thought that because of my lack of experience, I didn't necessarily have much to bring to such a revolutionary group. My background is in administrative assistant things, and Tony, at our first meeting, told me, "OMG. We really need someone to help with our doodle polls and keeping our shit organized!" My job at the time was doing program evaluation, and I was desperate for more radical work, so getting to support a people's performance evaluation of the police was truly a dream.

MOLLY: As Ricardo mentioned, he pointed out that we were approaching the 150th anniversary of the Minneapolis Police Department during a meeting the two of us were having about ongoing work regarding the intersection of trauma and organizing. I walked away from that meeting with questions circulating, but what stood out was the way it felt to imagine a hopeful future. I tend to view responsibility as serious and necessary work. This challenged me to consider if responsibility also includes being a part of creating space for envisioning and revisioning our future world. And how that, too, is necessary work.

FIRST STEPS: What sparked this idea, and how did that spark grow into something specific?

RICARDO: I reached out to a few activists to run the idea by them and the response was enthusiastic. At first, people came to meet with me one-on-one, but soon folks who had gotten the overview from me were initiating people they knew. I wrote up a concept sheet that could be shared with potential recruits. At this time it was understood that we would begin the work with person-to-person recruitment and no public profile in order to keep the police from getting wind of it and initiating their own commemoration.

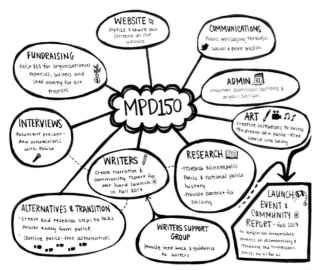

A visual chart showing different ways for new folks to plug into MPD150's work.

ARIANNA: The first thing that we talked about was who else we could contact that would be interested in supporting this or being involved. I thought of a few different organizers, a few former mentors, even one of my professors from college (who ended up being one of the first people to get a stack of reports when they were ready).

The question was, *"What do we want this to look like and who do we want to bring in?"* We wanted to make sure that we were developing a model of work that's really different. We wanted to make sure that the project was going to be sustainable and that it was going to be really lateral—that anyone who needed to take a break could, and the work would go on. And to have it be okay.

RICARDO: Our first group meeting was in October 2016 at Boneshaker Books, organized via email invitations to people who had already had an initial conversation. The meeting started with finding out what had brought people there, exploring the concept and strategy, defining next steps, and choosing task forces to be part of. It was agreed that the project was unapologetically abolitionist in outlook, anchored in the history of slavery, racism, and class. It was also agreed that our report, whatever form it took, would be delivered to the communities, not aimed at policy-makers, the media, or the police.

It was also decided that we would be a grouping of individuals, not a coalition of organizations. Members of other groups were welcome but organizations could not join. It was noted that we were not forming a new permanent grouping, but rather seizing the moment to change the political chemistry around policing. Our hope was that we would be able to steer clear of past rivalries, turf jealousies, and other baggage attached to existing organizations. An initial discussion was held about security, access to shared documents, etc. Tori took on a coordinating role at that stage, posting meeting notes, coordinating meetings, etc. That role would pass to others at later stages.

What really struck me at that time was the observation that people came into this project leaving their egos behind. There was a great deal of openness and listening rather than grandstanding or jockeying for leadership or status.

People divided into task forces around fundraising, interviews, and research, primarily. Social media and other publicity was not yet relevant.

NIKKI: I remember who was in the room, where we were. I remember the brilliant minds gathered at our first meeting at Boneshaker. I remember feeling connected and inspired. There were a lot of folks that were on the edge of burnout, if not in full burnout mode.

It was clear that we needed to be shifting energy away from only putting out fires and into something that gave us hope, that felt empowering and responsive vs. solely reactive.

We agreed right away that we would focus on narrative, that we were not the group that was going to be directly shifting policy. I remember wondering in the beginning how that was going to go.

MOLLY: The meeting at Boneshaker Books was full of powerful organizers and leaders—activists, artists, tech-minded folks, and truth tellers. We were each asked to identify our skills and imagine what our role in a project like this could be. The room was full, and there were so many people who were not in it. That thread has continued to weave through our work together. We have a core team of brilliant minds and there is also so much community brilliance dedicated to other ongoing work. This work is a piece of the larger framework. It became clear early on that we would focus on vision and narrative shifting. People spoke to how significant it would be if police abolition became a part of the broader municipal and national conversation. I think we're seeing that happen more and more now. The conversation is shifting to what Black, brown, and Indigenous voices have been calling for for years.

TONY: When I came on board, we knew that the idea was some kind of report, but it was still relatively unclear what that report would look like. We had discussed the possibility of a report card, interviews, and historical content, but still weren't sure how long it would be, what information it would contain, etc. When the soft launch happened, I think we started structuring out the report a lot more. The workgroups, particularly History, Interviews, and Alternatives/Transition, started to figure out exactly what they wanted their final products to look like, and how much space it would require. Then I think the rest sort of fell into place as we set a date for the report and scrambled to get it done on time.

ARIANNA: We also started talking with some of the bigger community players right away. That's when Voices for Racial Justice got pulled in; they were hosts of ours right away, and they continue to support our work. Of the first group of twenty or so people who we pulled in, maybe five of those folks ended up becoming a part of the core team, but everyone else was making suggestions of people to contact. It was a lot of information-gathering about how to do this really quickly because the need and the want were there; we just wanted to make sure it was sustainable... and that we got the upper hand. And we did.

SHEILA: I came in maybe a month before the launch event. The research team was finishing up their work, and we were trying to get all of the writing done for the report, while also planning this big launch event. Things were honestly pretty bananas, but what struck me when I first got involved was how much laughter was in the meeting.

I absolutely did not expect that when joining a group that was researching the history of police violence and failed reform. It was the beginning of my understanding of what police abolition really means, which is thinking about what we need to create a healthy, safe, joyful world. I also learned about the deep importance of snacks and cinnamon tea when under a tight deadline.

JAE HYUN: Because I came in later than the rest of the group, and wasn't already in people's organizing circles, I had different initial steps to getting involved. And I definitely had moments of feeling like the new kid; so much work had been done and I had a more limited view of what that grounding felt like in real time. After I submitted the online interest form I initially had a one-to-one with Martin, then met with the other folks focused on fundraising. From there I just started going to core meetings and plugging in where I could.

An interactive activity at the "Making It Real" exhibit asking participants to recall their experiences with police, color-coded by neighborhood.

131

DOING THE WORK:
During those early days, what was the approach? How were decisions made?

NIKKI: Decisions were typically made collectively, by consensus. I feel like consensus was fairly smooth to obtain in the group, even with people coming in and out. There were some sticky things that came up, of course, but we were able to work through most of them in respectful ways. I think our guiding principles really helped give us a strong foundation.

TONY: I loved that everyone was committed to working cooperatively, and that no one "owned" the project. It felt very powerful to me as an anarchist and recent émigré from an organization with lots of problematic power dynamics. From a philosophical perspective, the idea was always that the process was more important than the product, and that we should prioritize people's sustainability over their productivity. People were invited to step in and out of the project as they needed to, and many did. To make sure that the work continued anyway, we kept up bi-weekly, then weekly, core team meetings where we could identify what big work needed to happen and what decisions needed to be made, along with the workgroup meetings where work actually happened.

Decisions were usually made by the folks more directly connected to the decision (e.g. interview group members making decisions about which interviews should be included), with bigger decisions being made by the core team via a consensus decision-making model. In those cases, someone would usually bring up a partnership opportunity, challenge, or idea to the group, and we would chat about it for as long as we needed to to create consensus. Where there wasn't consensus, we didn't move forward with the idea.

Maybe the most salient version of this was when we were trying to decide if we wanted to respond to meeting invites from the Mayor and Police Chief. We discussed our options for quite a while, and though some members were open to it, we decided that MPD150 wouldn't get involved in policy work. And that, to me, was great decision making: individual members were welcome to chat with policy makers (but not cops), but we collectively decided that MPD150 wasn't the right container for that work. And I think it was the right decision.

MARTIN: Tasks were divided out into working groups, which had a rotating cast of folks working in them as their availability allowed. Detailed decisions got made by the people close to the related work, and larger decisions were made by the core group. This worked well in a lot of ways, as it made room for everyone to contribute and have some level of control over decisions, while keeping the detailed decisions from becoming larger than they needed to be and making sure the right people had the right input.

On the other hand, the drawback to not having a clear leader is that some folks are simply willing to speak up more than others, which led to some moments of minor conflict. Overall, though, I think that system of decision making worked well for us and we managed to keep everyone's voices involved.

ARIANNA: There was a core team, but it wasn't a closed core team—it was a "right now" core team. It was a "do you have time for this? Is this something you want to be doing?" core team. And other folks were doing complimentary work (art, history, a group that was looking into a film project, etc.). So they would report in, and that made it easy to delegate tasks out that way... which isn't something I've found in other organizing, where there are a lot of folks who end up looking at things from a top-down perspective, and need to have control over every moving piece.

MOLLY: From the beginning, people were focused on getting the work done. We were on a somewhat short timeline. There is a lot to consider in this work and many of us were coming in with different philosophies. This work itself didn't build broad community power, but it did distill a history and narrative that could be used to build power. One thing that stood out to me was how decisions were made. At meetings, we would talk in depth about certain aspects of the work as well as how it fits into the broader context. There were many times we did not agree. Sometimes in big ways, sometimes in smaller ways. We always led the conversation back to getting things done. What's trendy in an activist world isn't always aligned with what's grounded and accessible. That continues to be true. There were times I walked away from meetings frustrated, but what kept me coming back was the mutual respect in the room and the absolute commitment to getting the work done.

RICARDO: I don't recall explicitly setting out a formal decision-making process. Our practice was to weigh the possible ideas and come to agreement collectively. I would say that it was understood that a unified group was more important in most cases than winning a particular decision. We also set up security protocols, a tactical statement [see p.73], and came to affirm some more general attitudes—for example, that people should participate to the level that felt sustainable, could pull back as necessary, and rejoin when possible. It was also emphasized that anyone who could not fulfill a commitment should either pass it on to someone else, or let the group know so that it would not fall through the cracks. Continued recruitment was also on our radar, with care to think about whose involvement would be useful given the stage we were at, which called for patience and discretion.

DOING THE WORK (Pt. 2): Describe the process of creating and distributing the report itself.

RICARDO: The MPD150 process unfolded in stages, each marked by a public event. The initial stage of under-the-radar research, interviewing, and recruiting lasted until May, 2017. At that time we met with Shay Berkowitz, representing a radical family foundation, the Still Ain't Satisfied Fund (co-led by Phyllis Wiener and Maya Wiener Berkowitz), who convinced us that in order to effectively fundraise we would need a higher profile—and that in any case, the MPD was not equipped to counter what we were doing. This led to planning for an invitation-only "soft launch" at CTUL (Centro de Trabajadores Unidos en Lucha), in August. Using a creative format suggested by Arianna, we set up tables around the areas of work, had members share how we each had been attracted to the project, and let people circulate to the task force tables that attracted them. This expanded our outreach and allowed us to crowd-source fundraising to match a grant from the Still Ain't Satisfied Fund. It also inaugurated our social media presence and the creation of zines.

TONY: At the soft launch, we set the goal of releasing a report before the end of the year, with the workgroups and core team and writers working together to identify what needed to happen to meet that goal.

RICARDO: Our next major landmark was the launch itself in November 2017, also at CTUL, at which three hundred people packed the hall for a creative presentation of the report—which had been rushed into production to meet the deadline. This was followed by a growing number of conference appearances, classroom and workshop presentations, merchandise, and the production of an audiobook version of the report.

SHEILA: At our launch event, the presenters were not just core group members. We did a cabaret-style event where we had people who had been involved in MPD150, in ways big or small, perform poems, share history and findings from the report, sing songs, and offer proposals for the next steps in dismantling the Minneapolis Police Department, along with space for the 300+ audience members to talk with each other. It truly felt like an event created with, and for, community.

KYLE: The launch was a pretty incredible event. The poetry, the music, the conversation (and the turnout!)—it was cool to see so many people energized by the work. That being said, it was also a stressful day. The original run of the report had printed with a cover photo that prominently featured a community member's face. Because of the rush toward the end of the process (a major lesson learned: *don't put yourself in the position to have to rush*), we hadn't had a chance to notice or discuss that. The community member raised some concerns, so we, on the day of the launch, printed a few hundred "alternate cover" stickers, and a bunch of us applied them to the first big batch of reports as people arrived at the event.

RICARDO: A year after the launch, we opened an art exhibit at New Rules on the North Side, which featured illustration panels of the report, commissioned art, and panels and discussions. The panel discussions were made up of leaders and activists who were not MPD150 members, in line with our strategy of expanding alliances and buy-in, rather than taking up the spotlight. After each of these events, we met to assess and set the stage for the next period. In January 2019, we held a community council of allies to help us evaluate where we'd been and what to do next. In a group meeting after that, we decided to embark on a final year of the project, initiating projects that would extend the impact of our work past our organizational sunset.

Less public moments of significance included our decision not to issue public statements in the wake of police crimes; to remain purely narrative in nature and not engage in policy proposals; to redefine ourselves from a general membership organization to a collective in order to prevent being overwhelmed by white volunteers; and to set a time at which the organization as such would cease to exist.

MOLLY: How do you strike a balance of naming and honoring those who have been doing this work for generations, all of the questions that may arise as we move towards abolition, all of the moments in the history of policing that exist in the pain and grief of Black, brown and Indigenous people, and make it something that can be shared and read reasonably quickly? Those are questions we're still asking. Kyle, Felicia, Ricardo, Sheila, Tony, UyenThi, and others who wrote and designed content, FAQs, shareable images, and info sheets did amazing work.

The report itself focused on constructing a timeline of policing and reforms grounded in the present work of community members following the murders of Terrance Franklin, Fong Lee, Jamar Clark, and Justine Damond in Minneapolis. The future section talks about what we already have, what people have created to take care of each other, and asks us to consider what we need to continue to create.

I think the most valuable part of that is how clearly the future section illustrates that it is a matter of perspective and priorities. After years of organizing and narrative shifting by so many BIPOC voices, people can no longer say a future without police is not possible.

LESSONS LEARNED: The Process

KYLE: I'm super excited about the possibility of people in other cities replicating this work—diving into the history of their police departments, and working to change the narrative around safety, policing, and what healthy communities look like. I'm also thinking about how important it will be for that work to not be a linear, one-to-one copy of ours, since every community is different. For example, we were able to pay our writers and researchers, because we exist in a community in which there are both funding opportunities for weird, radical work like this, and qualified, cool people to do it. That landscape will look different in different places, and the approaches may have to shift.

JAE HYUN: Having a clear scope for the project worked well. I came in after this had been established, and it was something that would get brought back up as we were making other decisions after the exhibit, including when we decided to sunset.

NIKKI: One of the biggest things I appreciated about this group was the ability for people to move in and out of the project. With a long-term project like this, it felt super important for people to be valued for what they were able to bring to the group when they were able to bring it. From my perspective, folks were always affirmed and supported in decisions to step out, to flow in and out as needed. It was asked that people do their best to be very clear about what they felt like they could contribute and what their capacity was. When there's a project with a lot of moving parts, we need to have clear communication. There was a lot of trust with the group that the work was being done, and things were moving along outside of our meeting and check in times.

UYENTHI: Like any group project, working alongside other humans can be challenging. I think this group did a pretty good job at keeping up good communication and accountability with each other.

Individuals would, for the most part, let each other know what their capacity was with certain projects, or if they needed to step back from the work and come back at a later time. I think that honesty and transparency really helped us keep it moving, even if we had to pause and re-convene a few weeks or months later.

TONY: Time-limited projects are an amazing way to limit burnout. I'm surprised at how much less tired I've been during periods when we were sprinting toward an end goal, as opposed to previous organizing efforts which were intended to go on indefinitely.

Allowing folks to step up and step back as their capacity required actually made us more resilient and sustainable, not less, because everyone felt a great deal of love and care for the project.

RICARDO: All that being said, in the final stages of report creation, and in the creation and coordination of the exhibit, we left key people insufficiently supported and having to take on too much of the burden of ensuring successful outcomes.

LESSONS LEARNED:
Security

MARTIN: Nothing we did for this project was illegal, so security concerns weren't our highest priority. That said, we did a fair amount of things to limit who had access to real resources (the website, money, community interviews before names were either cleared or removed, ect). This was mostly to ensure if we had anything that could have put someone in danger, or put the project at risk, it was in the hands of people we knew and trusted. Knowing who was in the room was important, and knowing what our group policy was as far as public engagement helped here as well. But, as has been said above, since we were focused on narrative work and didn't have any direct actions or the like, our risk level was pretty low.

TONY: By choosing an organizing modality that wasn't centered on illegal action, we were able to reduce most of the risks of infiltration or prosecution. Even if the cops had come after us (and we had contingency plans if they did), it would have ultimately been a public relations defeat for them. Doing our organizing out in the open made it more difficult for them to counter effectively.

LESSONS LEARNED:
Fundraising

MARTIN: Early on, I wasn't entirely clear on what the scope of the work I was expected to do was, particularly considering doing financial work for a group without a clear definition of who was allowed to spend money or where it was coming from. I attribute this more to my own familiarity with hierarchical organizations and more rigid structures than the group's setup. After being involved for a bit and figuring out how our finances were going to work, I came up with systems for myself—both to keep people informed, and try to control the flow of money in a responsible and consensus driven way so that the work wouldn't get held up by that constraint.

ARIANNA: I would encourage folks to apply for fellowships and grants a lot more. A few of us applied for Soros, for Headwaters, for other things. Some we got; some we didn't. It is really time-consuming to do grant writing; that is the unfortunate part. But that is one of the fundraising things that I wish that we would have had more support from folks in community to do, in hindsight: grant writing. We also found some really awesome pots of money from folks trying to redistribute wealth. I also wish we would have had something more concretely organized for finding "secret white people money." I will say: money never felt like a problem, or a stress; money was never at the core of this. It's something I've thought a lot about: I really wish we could have done the film project we discussed, but we needed $20,000 to do that. But that's what I mean: dream really, really big and keep pushing for that.

NIKKI: Being able to have paid workers at times for larger-scale deadlines was crucial. We got better at checking in with each other about making sure needs were met and people felt valued for their work. We need each other to stick around and sometimes that looks like paying folks for their brilliance.

MARTIN: We benefited quite a bit from the availability of grant funding for strange radical projects like ours in Minneapolis. That might not be a resource that's available everywhere, so being inventive with how you get funding is useful. We did a couple of online crowd-funding campaigns, and while they were effective, it was clear you can only do that so many times before people are burnt out on it. House parties, events, and direct asks were also effective—both at fundraising, and at increasing community engagement and awareness.

TONY: We chose not to host administrative staff, and only hired folks for time-limited project work. This meant that fundraising took up relatively little time, but we could still benefit from the increased capacity of having full-time workers. We also had two paid workers dealing with outside issues step back from the project unexpectedly. Being careful about hiring in a context without administrative oversight is important, and requires a lot of trust.

Also, fundraisers hosted by friends and group members were very useful both for raising money and for creating more public awareness around the project. Grants were also incredibly helpful, as we asked for support for work we had ongoing, rather than developing projects to take advantage of grant opportunities.

LESSONS LEARNED:
Outreach and Promotion

TONY: Remember: if the content isn't accessible to folks without a college education, it's not powerful.

The tools that are the most accessible are those that get used the most. It's far easier to get people to become abolitionists than you would think. The way you present the narrative depends on who you're speaking to—leftists, liberals, conservatives, police—but there's a way to speak to it that's accessible to almost everyone. Don't be afraid to be strategic about which narratives around abolition you deploy in which places.

KYLE: Writing the report was a lot of work; getting people to read the report was also a lot of work. I think we've done a good job allocating resources to both sides of that framework. We've had a consistent social media presence, managed by people who actually understand how Instagram, Twitter, and Facebook work (something a lot of activist groups struggle with). Those channels are places we can plug the report, but

COFFEE WITH AN ABOLITIONIST
WHAT DOES A POLICE-FREE WORLD LOOK LIKE?

Meet with members of MPD150 to chat about police abolition and what we mean when we envision a police-free future.

Various dates and locations throughout MPLS.

they're also places we can spotlight all kinds of other resources, campaigns in other cities, and beyond—social media, when it's done right, can be a powerful platform for political education, discussion, and community-building.

We've also had numerous well-attended, well-organized events to keep our profile up. We've had a media strategy, including traditional press releases and letters-to-the-editor, alongside email blasts, fundraising campaigns, and all the other tools that keep work fresh in people's heads. We created an audio reading of the entire report. We've also had a website that, aside from our own materials, features a big, powerful bank of articles and readings for people who want to learn more. That can help drive people to the website for years to come.

SHEILA: A challenge in this sort of anniversary-based project was the question of what to do after the report was out, when the anniversary year was over. We knew we wanted to get it into the hands of as many people as possible in Minneapolis and around the country, in classrooms and living rooms, and on the streets, but we didn't necessarily have a structured dissemination plan. That plan emerged over time, and also brought in new mediums (we turned the report into an audiobook and an art exhibit), but I think it would have been helpful to have more of that dissemination plan mapped out ahead of time so that we could help spread out folks' capacity after the sprint of getting the report finished, and bring on new people as some folks needed to cycle off after the research and writing were done.

RICARDO: The continual use of different communication channels and methods—printed report, zines, videos, exhibit, audiobook, social media platforms, workshop and classroom outlines—provided opportunities for wider exposure and engagement.

MARTIN: In terms of outreach, one thing to keep in mind is who you have in the room. It's incredibly easy to get a room full of white liberals in Minneapolis. With a project like this, addressing issues that affect BIPOC communities so much more directly, it's important to make sure the right voices are given room to speak.

KYLE: On one hand, it's important that the work isn't entirely driven by people who are not the primary targets of police violence. On the other, though, it's important to make use of the energy and resources that that demographic brings to the table, so that the burden is not 100% on poor communities of color to do everything all the time. That's a balancing act.

When we pay writers, designers, visual artists, and researchers, that process creates space for ensuring that there's real representation beyond tokenism. The money itself expands the pool of who has access to getting involved, too; it's not just well-off, white twenty-somethings or whatever.

Having robust fundraising efforts also creates spaces for those white liberals to plug in and contribute to the project in a meaningful way. They can bring us to their churches or colleges, or donate to help cover printing costs, or show up to events to learn more and then take that knowledge into their peer groups.

MOLLY: In this work and in any work, it is necessary to continually ask who is represented and who we are making the work accessible to. That was my biggest concern from the beginning. Do I think we succeeded in reaching everyone we needed to reach? No. Do I think that we created a tools and resources that can reach the people we need to reach? Yes.

LESSONS LEARNED:
Narrative Organizing

NIKKI: I appreciated staying with our commitment to be a narrative-focused group. There were a lot of opportunities to speak to local politicians, police, and other people in power about police reform. In the moment, that would seem very tempting, but I valued our ability to stay focused on our work and trust that there were other groups and communities in the Twin Cities who were better suited to take on those roles.

KYLE: Because we were pretty clear from the beginning that MPD150's work would be about narrative-shifting, and not necessarily the nuts-and-bolts of policy-changing, that also has positioned us in a useful way—we're not the "leaders" or primary catalysts of building a police-free Minneapolis; that work will be driven by larger movements of the people most impacted by the issues. We're just contributing some resources, some tools, and some perspective. Other organizations and entities, from neighborhood groups, to city council campaigns, and beyond, can run with it.

RICARDO: This work felt different from much organizing because it was built around a really big goal presented as not only practical, but inevitable. Having the report made clear that a future without police abolition would not be viable. It was hope-based, in other words, not reactive. I think that the support we got both internally and from outside was in part because we tried to model the world we were fighting for in how we centered grassroots community and treated each other humanely.

Patient work set on a shared purpose has paid off in the impact that our narrative shift strategy has had in local politics. This includes the interjection of police abolition as an issue in local elections even before the report was released, and the success of the Reclaim the Block coalition in shifting allocated funds away from the department. It has also contributed to increased resistance to police expansion proposals.

A narrative perspective on organizing is fundamental to shifting the balance of power. By targeting the very legitimacy of the police, we challenged what they have always seen as their strength and which they are not well prepared to defend.

The willingness of even resistant people to accept the possibility of police abolition—after a little discussion—was shocking. The turnout and response to the report launch was something we could foresee as a goal but I would have expected after five or more years of consistent work—not within a year of having started it!

TONY: Over the course of a year or two, we seriously shifted the narrative of the left in Minneapolis around policing. Projects like this, a deep dive into solutions around a given issue, have a real possibility of influencing leftist thought in a city and refining a narrative, as long as the people doing the project are well thought of by folks across the community.

An interactive activity at the "Making It Real" exhibit asking participants to consider where Minneapolis should invest its resources

137

Do you have any stories or memories from your work with MPD150 that might be illuminating, symbolic, or just cool to share?

UYENTHI: I've loved seeing how artists have contributed their creative work to this process. We designed a few simple t-shirts to help fundraise and plant this idea that a police-free world is possible, and did a call for artists to contribute designs. Through Arianna, I got connected with DeLesslin George-Warren (Catawba Nation), who contributed a design that read "There was a time before police and there will be a time after." Via the artist statement: the design was "created using an image from a 2017 protest on the National Mall in Washington, D.C., where tribes literally occupied the Capital using structures that pre-date the formation of the United States. Although DeLesslin's tribe did not and does not use tipi, Catawbas are one of the many, many communities that existed before the advent of violent policing and we will be one of the many communities that survive it. A better world is possible because a better world has existed."

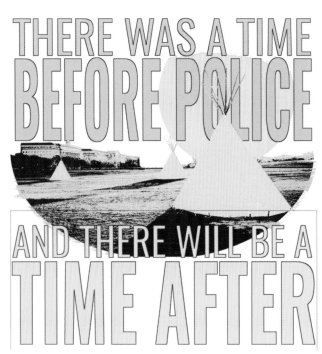

Image: Delesslin George-Warren

TONY: Two stories come to mind: one is when the organization Pollen released their voter guide, and a ton of city council and mayoral candidates said that they could envision living in a Minneapolis without police. That was a few months before we released the report, and we could already tell that the conversations we were having were making an impact, and that the report would just cement it.

The second is when I talked to a person who was doing research on police abolition across the country, maybe six months after the release of the report. They mentioned that they had interviewed some abolitionists from Oakland, the home of Critical Resistance and other incredible abolition work, and that they had asked them the question, "where do you think the police will be abolished first?" They answered "Minneapolis," and in that moment I was sure that we would. Not today, or tomorrow, but someday.

NIKKI: There were so many times in random conversations that people would bring up MPD150 and the idea of abolition. It was cool of course to hear random people talking about a group they didn't know I was part of, but more importantly, it showed that our work was igniting conversations and imaginations around the Twin Cities. There is also an amazing group called Reclaim the Block that began in 2018 who works to organize the Minneapolis community and city council members to shift money from the police department into other areas that promote community health and safety. It's really encouraging to see other police abolition and reform work sprout up throughout the Twin Cities over the past three years.

RICARDO: The Reclaim the Block campaign around police funding is a good example of what we hoped for: on-the-ground organizing independent of us but obviously fed and inspired by our narrative framing and making ample use of the research and analysis in the report.

KYLE: My work puts me in touch with a lot of people who are new to the idea of abolition, and our "frequently asked questions" zine has been super useful. Right away, on the very first interior page, it clearly, concisely lays out the argument that "*Police abolition work is not about snapping our fingers and magically defunding every department in the world instantly. Rather, we're talking about a process of strategically reallocating resources, funding, and responsibility away from police and toward community-based models of safety, support, and prevention.*"

That argument, at least in my experience, is really persuasive for people who might otherwise be suspicious or outright hostile to the idea. The logic is difficult to argue with. We should invest in the organizations and structures that prevent harm, not just punish harm after it happens.

Whether people read the whole report, or have a deep understanding of the roots of policing, I think that argument is a key piece of really shifting the narrative, and it's deeply related to encouraging systems thinking around other issues too, from sexual assault prevention, to the climate crisis, and beyond. How do we pivot? How do we make sure that we're not just "doing good work," but doing the work that means that we don't have to still be doing the same work fifty years from now? I think MPD150 has asked these questions in a very elegant way, and that people are more open to new, visionary, radical answers now than I've ever seen.

MARTIN: I have been in school for the duration of this project. Shortly after the report was published, I had a class that was focusing on political movements around the globe. During the unit on movements focused on criminal justice in the United States, our professor used the MPD150 report as an optional reading, and had copies available for the entire class. I'm not sure how many read it, but seeing something that we worked on, and particularly the topic of police abolition, brought up in a college classroom was an incredible feeling and really highlighted the potential impact of this type of narrative work. I know at least a few students from that class attended our exhibit launch event.

ARIANNA: Some of my favorite memories are us eating together all the time. In the final days of finishing the report, I had brought over wine and chocolate because we were... there was a reason we were going to be having an exceptionally long night—we all knew it. So I brought that, and it was the one photo I took from the early crew. And I was just happy about it, I don't want to forget this; this is something that is really special.

I remember our launch event: there was a point where we actually had to turn people away; the building was completely packed, even the overflow room in the basement. And I remember getting numbers about how many people were watching the stream online, and I'm like "holy shit." Looking at the Unicorn Riot stream the next day, there were something like over 2,000 individual viewers. It was incredible to see that, to see the interest. And I know that because of all this, we pushed this conversation forward in Minneapolis; the 2017 mayoral candidates had to answer a question about this work, and it's still a part of the conversation. And we absolutely made space for silliness and joy.

MOLLY: Our work is not done, but the work we came together to do as a group has been completed. We evaluated the 150-year history of policing in Minneapolis, presented a comprehensive report of historical events, cycles of reforms, and the resources that exist and need to be created, collaborated with artists to host an exhibit, and created resources for pop ed. The vision for a police-free future exists, the argument for abolition has been clearly laid out, and now it's time to do the work of building and dismantling.

SHEILA: In 2019, it was two years after the report had been released; we had presented tons of workshops, friendraisers in people's living rooms, school visits, tabling at street fairs, etc. I was sitting in Minneapolis City Hall, and someone got up to testify during the city budget hearing about a proposed $9M increase in the police budget. And in the beginning of their testimony they said, *"I want to thank MPD150; their report has taught me more about policing and the history of the Minneapolis Police Department than I ever knew."* And then this person continued on to demand that the city council divest from the police department and invest in housing, opioid response, and meeting people's basic needs. And this is someone whom I had never met before (the Minneapolis radical scene isn't that big). And in that moment I thought, *"this is it; this is the point of this work."* It's about getting people to learn that history in a powerful way, and taking that knowledge to the people in power and demanding that we start dismantling MPD one million at a time!

"we are bending the future, together, into something we have never experienced. a world where everyone experiences abundance, access, pleasure, human rights, dignity, freedom, transformative justice, peace. we long for this, we believe it is possible."[1] - adrienne maree brown

1   maree brown, adrienne. "All Organizing is Science Fiction." Arts in a Changing America. October 18, 2016. Accessed November 14, 2017. https://artsinachangingamerica.org/nyc-launch-highlight-the-response/.

These are some of the individuals and groups (in no order) that have been part of this effort to date. Blank spaces represent individuals who have chosen to not make their participation public:

MPD150 is grateful to:

Shay Berkowitz, Phyllis Wiener, and Still Ain't Satisfied: A Foundation with Attitude for a grant and matching challenge gift; many individual supporters—including contributors to our online fundraising campaign and at fundraising events; and Voices for Racial Justice, for being our fiscal sponsor.

Katherine Parent
Rica Highers
Erin Bogle
Kyle Tran Myhre
Ricardo Levins Morales
Olivia Levins Holden
Betty Tisel
Jonathan Stegall
Arianna Nason
Rachel Mueller
Sheila Nezhad
See More Perspective
Juliana Hu Pegues
Essie Schlotterbeck
Erica Josefina Vibar Sherwood
Asfia Rizwy
Ashley Fairbanks
Tori Hong
Tony Williams
Chaun Webster
Teresa Zaffiro
Nikki Fleck
Phillip Otterness
Maryama Dahir
Sex Worker Outreach Project Minneapolis
Northside Research Team
Vina Kay

Molly Glasgow
Paige Ingram
RadAzns
Behind The Blue Line
Rose Todaro
Martin Sheeks
Gretchen Hovan
Annabelle Marcovici
caspian wirth-petrik
Octavia Smith
eunha jeong wood
Leilah Abdennabi
D. Robinson
Lena K. Gardner
M. Nichole Day
UyenThi Tran Myhre
Peter VanKoughnett
Jae Hyun Shim

_____
_____
_____
_____
_____
_____
_____
_____
_____

Special Thanks To:
Printer (for first edition): Smart Set
Designer: Ashley Fairbanks
Additional Design: Felicia Pruitt Brown
Photos: Ryan Stopera & Annabelle Marcovici